# SMARTER LIVING

# SMARTER LIVING

## WORK · NEST · INVEST · RELATE · THRIVE

**KAREN BARROW, TIM HERRERA, KARRON SKOG**
and the reporters at *The New York Times*

BLACK DOG
& LEVENTHAL
PUBLISHERS
NEW YORK

Black Dog & Leventhal Publishers
Hachette Book Group
1290 Avenue of the Americas
New York, NY 10104

www.hachettebookgroup.com
www.blackdogandleventhal.com

First Edition: December 2019

Black Dog & Leventhal Publishers is an imprint of Perseus Books, LLC, a subsidiary of
Hachette Book Group. The Black Dog & Leventhal Publishers name and logo are
trademarks of Hachette Book Group, Inc.

The publisher is not responsible for websites (or their content) that are not owned
by the publisher.

The Hachette Speakers Bureau provides a wide range of authors for speaking events.
To find out more, go to www.HachetteSpeakersBureau.com or call (866) 376-6591.

Print book interior design by Joanna Price

Library of Congress Cataloging-in-Publication Data

Names: Barrow, Karen, author. | Skog, Karron, author.
Title: Smarter living: work – nest – invest – relate – thrive / Karen
Barrow, Tim Herrera, Karron Skog, and the reporters at The New York Times.
Description: First Edition. | New York, NY: Black Dog & Leventhal
Publishers, [2019]
Identifiers: LCCN 2019011727| ISBN 9780762494125 (hardcover) | ISBN
9780762494118 (ebook)
Subjects: LCSH: Lifestyles. | Sustainable living. | Success. | Happiness.
Classification: LCC HQ2042 .B37 2019 | DDC 646.7—dc23
LC record available at https://lccn.loc.gov/2019011727

Printed in China

1010

10 9 8 7 6 5 4 3 2 1

# CONTENTS

# Invest  96

# Relate  138

# Thrive 180

# INTRODUCTION

**LET'S GET THIS OUT OF THE WAY** nice and early: You will not find the definitive answers to all of life's problems and mysteries in this book.

Phew. Glad we covered that.

The easiest way to tell you what you are going to find in the following five chapters is to tell what you won't find: prescriptive, end-of-conversation, "this is the only solution you'll ever need" type of advice and guidance. If you ever see a book selling you the one answer to all of your problems, put it down immediately and walk away. There is no one-size-fits-all answer to any of our problems, much less the complicated, messy, personal, impactful and important ones we cover in this book.

Now that the pressure's off, let us explain what you will find in this book.

Smarter living.

Smarter Living, the guidance and advice section of *The New York Times* from which this book was created, tries to tackle life's problems from a better point of view. The five chapters in this book—which cover your home; your work life; your health; your finances; and your relationships (with others and with yourself)—are written not by so-called "self-help experts," "productivity hackers," "gurus," "ninjas" or "rock stars" of any sort. They're written by hardworking, rigorous journalists who are regular people first and deal with the same everyday issues that you do, and who are also looking for solutions.

for answers that drives Smarter Living, and that's what drives this book.

But this book isn't all how to's and step-by-step guides. Alongside thoughtful, well-reasoned

> ❝
> *Our goal was to cover the spectrum of modern life, and regardless of where you are in your journey on this planet, there is something for you in these pages.*

Let's look at one of our favorite stories in this book: "How to Be an Ace Salary Negotiator (Even if You Hate Conflict)" from the Work chapter:

Written by A. C. Shilton, this story coaches you on everything you may need to advocate for yourself during a salary negotiation—with the understanding that there's likely nothing in the world you'd less like to do than negotiate your salary for a new job. (Yes, it is a nightmare, we agree.)

This story is a perfect example of the Smarter Living ethos: a fully reported, wonderfully written piece of journalism born out of the author's own fear of negotiating her salary. A. C. was the perfect journalist to write that story because it was an issue that personally impacted her life and gave her the insight and clarity to approach the problem from the common perspective. She picked up on the issues and ideas that a "career coach" wouldn't even know to address. It's this fundamental curiosity and desire

stories advising you on everything from your 401(k) allocation to stain removal are emotional, relatable stories on dealing with anxiety, overcoming the unconscious biases that affect us every day, and small things you can do now to live a happier life. (Hint: Treat yourself like a friend.)

Our goal was to cover the spectrum of modern life, and regardless of where you are in your journey on this planet, there is something for you in these pages. In building this book, we pored over thousands of *New York Times* stories to find the absolute best of the best advice, and we couldn't be prouder of this collection.

All that said: Smarter Living is nothing without its readers! And we want to hear from you. Tweet your best tips for living smarter—whatever that looks like for you—using the hashtag #smarterliving.

We're all in this together, figuring it out as we go and trying to live smarter every day.

# Work

## CAREER MAINTENANCE · TIME MANAGEMENT AND PRODUCTIVITY · OFFICE LIFE

**NAVIGATING OUR LIVES** at work has never been more difficult. Technology has changed the way we do our jobs in ways we don't even understand, and the need to be "always-on" has forced work to seep into our personal lives and challenge our concept of the work-life balance. This is all on top of the normal work stuff we've dealt with for years: work friends, burning out, asking for a raise and sometimes just getting through the day.

Figuring out how to thrive at work is never easy, but read on and you'll have all the tools you'll need.

**IN THE FOLLOWING PAGES, YOU'LL LEARN HOW TO:**

- Beat burnout and get back to being your best work self

- Ask for a raise—even if just thinking about that fills you with dread

- Deal with all kinds of bosses

- Become productive at work instead of just being "busy"

- Take a nap on the job (and justify it!)

# How to Manage Your Career

BY KEVIN GRANVILLE

**THERE IS NO SHORTAGE OF BOOKS,** podcasts and motivational speakers claiming to reveal the secret truth behind successful careers. The bottom line of most of these advice-givers? A successful career requires managing the person in the mirror: overcoming your tendencies and habits that can undermine efforts to find happiness at work.

## FIRST, BUILD A SOLID FOUNDATION

Whether you want to start a new career, grow where you are or simply create a safety net for your future, there are two main things you should always be doing for your career: networking and learning.

Networking has an awful reputation. It conjures up images of self-absorbed corporate ladder-climbers whose main interest is "What's in it for me?"

But researchers almost unanimously agree that building and nurturing relationships with people—current and former colleagues and people we respect in the business—provides a strong medium for a vibrant career and a cushion for when the unplanned happens.

Networks provide a connection with fellow workers—an emotional link with those who know us. But they also provide a source of information or business intel—about your department, your business or your industry.

In fact, it is often the distant links in your networks that provide the most value—such as helping you find a job. The sociologist Mark Granovetter

**Take a leap.** Invite folks to drinks after work or to join you in a company-sponsored volunteer effort. The thing here is just getting to know people a bit better beyond working hours.

**Use social media.** LinkedIn and Facebook can provide an effective and relatively painless way to reach out to people you know, especially those who

> 66
>
> *Networks provide a connection with fellow workers— an emotional link with those who know us. But they also provide a source of information or business intel—about your department, your business or your industry.*

makes a distinction between strong ties (close friends, family, co-workers) and weak ties (former classmates, ex-colleagues, people we know but not well). In "The Strength of Weak Ties," he shows how these more distant links provide doorways into other networks we wouldn't normally have access to.

Here's how to think about nurturing your networking relationships:

**Start small.** When you run into a former co-worker at your place of business, say more than a quick hello. Try to take a moment and find out how they are doing. Jobs and responsibilities are always changing, and, frankly, it's nice when someone takes a sincere interest in our lives.

have changed jobs. Think of a colleague or classmate you've lost touch with, and make contact with a simple "what's new?" message. Relate a little (no more than a few sentences!) on what you've been up to, and ask how they've been doing.

Beyond managing your relationships, careers thrive when people keep up with changes in their fields. In every endeavor there are new technologies, new "best practices," changing regulations and previously unforeseen challenges. This applies to both the skilled mason and the architect of office towers. This is another way to keep building a solid career foundation.

Some ways to achieve this:

**Join a professional organization and attend their events.** Better yet, take part in different projects and help make presentations. You'll learn more about your field, gain experience, raise your profile and meet new people in your industry.

**Enroll in workshops and training sessions.** If they are offered at your workplace, these opportunities will expose you to something new, even if they don't always overlap with your current job.

**Continue your education by taking classes in your field.** There are several ways to do this, from the many free and relatively cheap courses online to attending a local brick-and-mortar school. Some labor unions, too, offer training. If you aren't sure what kind of course to take, ask co-workers or your supervisor. And be sure to check whether your employer can help underwrite the tuition. Many companies offer this benefit for classes that relate to your job. If this is an option, make sure your course plan satisfies your company's rules.

**Become the teacher.** If you have a special skill or knowledge, consider becoming an adjunct professor in your field at a college or university. Higher education institutions rely on adjuncts to teach professional courses. You'll earn some extra money and meet other adjuncts, who will give you new perspectives on your field.

## IMPROVING YOUR CURRENT SITUATION WITHOUT LEAVING

Let's say you have a job you like, but want to do even better and find a more prominent role in your organization, commensurate with your skills and interests. Or

perhaps you have a nagging feeling that you aren't being recognized for what you've brought to your team.

In a perfect universe, this sense of dissatisfaction would solve itself—the boss would recognize your efforts and potential, and you'd receive better assignments, a better work shift and a raise. But improving your situation at work will most likely require some proactive attention. It begins with a careful assessment of the person we're dealing with.

Start with a self-evaluation. Grab a piece of paper and jot down the following:

- Your strengths and weaknesses in your present job.
- Your skills and limitations.
- Your recent accomplishments and shortcomings.

Critical here is becoming aware of your own natural strengths and interests. You may already have a pretty firm grasp of them, or you may discover them as you piece together your self-assessment. If you are unsure, turn to a trusted colleague or former boss; their viewpoint will be especially valuable. You may look at your self-assessment and tell yourself, "Damn, I'm one of the best workers here, and nobody knows it!"

If so, it may be time to make a concentrated effort to raise your profile in the workplace. This will likely take some extra work. But here are a few suggestions, and none of them are backbreakers.

**Step up to solve problems.** You and your co-workers can probably come up with dozens of small (or large) processes that don't work for some reason—a software issue, a procedure issue, a deadline that no one can ever meet. But everyone is so busy that no one has time to find a solution. Make yourself that person. Odds are, the answer may simply involve getting the attention of the person in your organization who can address it.

**Suggest it.** Figure out how to make your department's work easier or better. Suggest it to your boss, and if she green-lights it, be ready to take the next step to make it a reality. Don't be hurt if your idea gets turned down; these things are like batting averages, and one out of three is excellent. The point is that you've made a stab at improving your workplace.

**Speak up.** Some people have absolutely no hesitation chattering away in group sessions and team meetings. Others have a natural reticence. If speaking in these settings doesn't come naturally, try to take a moment before the meeting to develop some questions. Some experts recommend trying to be the first person to speak up once the floor is opened up to questions—if only to quickly get the monkey off one's back.

Beyond raising your profile, it may be most strategic to flat out ask for a raise. What better way to improve your current situation?

Like a good lawyer about to argue a case, preparation is critical to improving your chances of success. From a variety of experts, here are some points to consider.

- First, do some research on salaries in your field. Data is available from different online sources (the Bureau of Labor Statistics compiles data for more than 800 occupations;

## WAYS TO MAKE YOUR ROLE MORE PROMINENT

Look for ways to solve a headache for your boss.

Offer to mentor new employees or coach co-workers about a new technology or tool.

Take on a task or work a shift that isn't exactly a favorite among the staff.

many other sites gather their data from different sources). Discussion of salaries can be difficult, but consider talking to colleagues or former co-workers. If you belong to a union and work according to a contract, check to see where you stand on the pay scales.

- Collect your "attaboy" and "attagirl" testimonials and complimentary comments from evaluations.
- Rehearse your arguments. Not just on paper, but speak them aloud. (Yes, it will help to have a friend play the boss.)
- Don't chicken out and make your request for a raise via email. Set up a meeting time with your boss and signal that it will be an important conversation.

Your attitude at the meeting is critical.

"You've got to go into these discussions with a clear sense that this is something you have earned, not a gift from your boss," said Kenneth N. Siegel, an industrial psychiatrist and president of the Impact Group, Inc., a leadership consulting firm.

If your boss says a pay raise is out of the question, either because of financial restrictions or your work doesn't merit it, here are some fallback positions:

- Offer to take on more responsibilities if that increases the chances of a raise.
- Propose agreeing to revisit the raise request at a future date, say in six months, when the company's finances may be more flexible.
- Consider asking for more vacation time, or a better work schedule, or broader training opportunities in place of a raise.
- Negotiate for a bonus or stock options.

## WHEN IT'S TIME TO GO

Sometimes a job is not working out and it's time to leave. Or the decision is made for you, and you've been laid off or fired. Or, after a period away from work to raise children or care for aging parents you are trying to re-enter the workforce. Each of these presents special challenges to keeping your career moving forward.

If leaving your job wasn't your choice—i.e., you were fired—you probably feel hurt, humiliated and angry. Getting fired, even from a job you didn't enjoy, is a kick in the gut. And a layoff, even one that's couched in language of "a numbers game," isn't

much better. Emotionally, it'll take a while to recover. So take that time to assess what went well and what didn't and what you want out of your next job. Then, get ready for the job search.

Once you're on the job hunt, your best resource will be—you guessed it—your network. The collection of people you know—and who know you—can provide intelligence about who might be hiring or even open doors and make a call for you.

Here are a few other things to remember:

**Customize your cover letter and résumé.** Do this for every job and company you apply to. This is a bit of flattery, but it also demonstrates your willingness to work for this job. Be aware, though, that varying your text presents additional opportunities for errors in grammar or spelling, so make sure to proofread your material several times.

**Make sure your online profiles are up to date with your latest skills.** Job recruiters often troll through these sites looking for qualified candidates.

**Get out and talk to people.** Reach out to people in the company or field where you want to work, ask about openings and how they got started. It's sometimes surprising what happens when you ask for some help. You will learn things, including whether the field you are thinking about is a good match.

**Be aware of age discrimination.** If you are nearing retirement age but still want to work, beware of the difficulties your age may pose. Age discrimination is tough to prove, but many older job seekers know it as a fact of life. To find a job that feels like a good fit—not like something that fit you 20 years ago—you might look for smaller organizations, including nonprofits, that will take advantage of your experience and expertise.

**Consider a career counselor.** If you are having a hard time getting back on your feet after a job loss, career counselors can help with résumé writing and career coaching. Fees vary, but expect private counselors to charge several hundred dollars for a few sessions. There are also free services offered through the Department of Labor's CareerOneStop services.

## CONSIDER GOING FREELANCE

As you consider your options, you may look to freelance or join the gig economy. For some, that can feel like an endless hamster wheel of low-paying work, scrambling to find the next gig to pay the bills. Others insist it is a realistic response to a new labor landscape, and that, handled well, it can provide a better life than working for a large organization and always fearing the next round of layoffs.

Before you decide, it helps to look at the pros and cons of independent work.

### In the pro column:

**A better home-life mix.** You can expect to have more control over your schedule when you work on-demand or freelance. This can feel liberating after the controlling schedules of life as an employee. A survey compiled by LinkedIn and Intuit found that 67 percent of freelance workers were satisfied or highly satisfied with their work-life balance.

## HIT THE PAUSE BUTTON

*As tempting as it may be to cut yourself loose from an unsatisfying job, there are several reasons to pause before submitting a resignation, according to Farai Chideya in her book The Episodic Career:*

Employers often practice "unemployment discrimination," preferring to hire candidates employed elsewhere rather than someone not in a job.

Your self-confidence (and bargaining position) as a job seeker will be higher if you are presently employed elsewhere.

It may make sense to wait it out. Organizations transition quickly these days, so a boss you don't get along with may be assigned elsewhere—or an appealing position in your organization may open up.

You'll have an easier time paying your bills while job searching if you are employed.

**A sense that you are in control of your life.** You may work just as hard, or harder, but it will be work that you will have chosen, rather than had imposed on you.

**Encourages an entrepreneurial view of life.** It will be to your advantage to explore and develop new ideas for work—to come up with ideas to use your skills, to be resourceful, to stay up late some nights planning the day ahead. Work will not be handed to you.

**For retirees, a source of extra income.** The gig economy has a lot of appeal for people who have retired from a traditional full-time job but still want some stimulation and a stream of money coming in.

of taking more control over your life—and that you could end up making more money and living a better life in the end. But transitions can be difficult.

**You'll lose corporate benefits you may have had.** Things like company contributions to health insurance, unemployment insurance, disability income, paid vacations and 401(k) matches will go away when you are on your own.

**You'll need to be disciplined with your schedule and finances.** A sense of the daily routine—which can be a creature comfort or a source of mind-numbing boredom—will be out the window. If you have two or

> 66
> *A sense of the daily routine—which can be a creature comfort or a source of mind-numbing boredom— will be out the window.*

## And on the con side:

**Your pay will be unpredictable.** The steady reliability of the same paycheck every pay period will disappear. You will have some great months and some not-so-great months. This will require some discipline in your spending.

**You may need to get used to a smaller income.** Becoming an independent worker may mean you'll need to scale back and consider living a simpler life. Advocates say this may be the temporary cost

more sources of work, all with different deadlines and time requirements, you'll need to become an expert at keeping a good schedule. The same goes for your finances and accounting. You'll need to keep good receipts for tax purposes. Keep track of payments— and get ready for a situation when you might have to demand payments when a customer is tardy.

**Fear of the unknown.** This is perhaps the biggest reason some people are repulsed by the independent-worker lifestyle. Will you be able to pay the bills? Will you be happy or miserable? The prospects may strike you as thrilling and life-affirming, or may keep you awake every night.

The best way to set up a gig-economy or freelance career is to make sure you always have work coming to you, so you don't have to go searching for the next paycheck. This comes from developing a reputation in your line of work. Some call this creating a brand.

(Wallflowers, step aside.)

"Many people don't want to deal with the hassle of a 'permanent career campaign,'" wrote Dorie Clark, the author of "Reinventing You." "They think it's too much work to contemplate their personal brand, maintain their social media footprint, or cultivate relationships when they're not on the make for a new job. Those are the people who will lose."

Think of your personal brand as simply letting people know who you are and what you do, and what work you have accomplished recently—through networking, personal contacts or a website. Remember, you are independent of the big corporation, and you should spend some part of your time drawing work to yourself. Being invisible isn't a good idea, or lucrative.

**The bottom line:** Pay attention to your career.

It sounds simple, but it's not so easy to follow, because we tend to confuse jobs and careers. Jobs demand so much of our time. But jobs are temporary, and are almost always in service of someone (or something) else.

But your career belongs to you alone, to nurture, steer, imagine and reimagine. No one else can do it for you.

Find the time to show your career some love. It'll be time well spent.

## RESOURCES FOR INDEPENDENT WORKERS

Remember, independent workers are not alone. There are ways to find advice, assistance and information.

The Freelancers Union, a nonprofit founded in 2003, provides advocacy and advice on a range of issues, including financial and insurance matters.

The consumer finance site NerdWallet has helpful articles that provide good background on what independent workers need to think about in terms of taxes, insurance and retirement.

Issues surrounding the gig economy are becoming more critical as a larger share of the workforce gets involved. If you want to keep up, the Workable Futures Initiative has done some significant research on this topic.

# How to Be an Ace Salary Negotiator (Even If You Hate Conflict)

BY A.C. SHILTON

**IN EVERY BOOK, BLOG OR CONFERENCE** about freelancing, you'll find the same piece of advice: Negotiate the fee on every assignment.

This is great advice. Or so I imagine; I wouldn't know.

In my 10 years of freelancing, I've never negotiated for a heftier fee. Not once. If a fee is too low, I'll simply decline the assignment and move on.

I might be paying for these financial transgressions for years—and salaried employees might be, too. Not negotiating the salary of your first job can cost you hundreds of thousands of dollars over the course of your career, according to Linda Babcock, an economics professor at Carnegie Mellon University and author of "Ask for It: How Women Can Use the Power of Negotiation to Get What They Really Want."

I've always pinned my poor negotiation skills on my aversion to conflict. But that's just an excuse; the truth is, I was just looking at negotiations from the wrong perspective. Here's how to stand up for your worth and walk away with more money.

## CONFLICT-AVERSE DOESN'T MEAN NEGOTIATION-AVERSE

When I explained my struggles to Dr. Babcock, her immediate response was: "Why are you thinking of a negotiation as a conflict?" She added that a negotiation should be a conversation, not a confrontation.

"If you see it as a conflict, and you're conflict-averse and avoid it, that's not going to serve you

Employers generally have a salary range, and if you're at the point in the interview or hiring process where it's time to discuss salary, it's absolutely worth your time and emotional investment to prod about wiggle room.

"If they've offered you a job, they want you to take that job," said Kimberly Churches, chief executive of the American Association of University Women

> **"**
>
> *Not negotiating the salary of your first job can cost you hundreds of thousands of dollars over the course of your career.*

well," she said. "Try seeing it as a conversation that needs to be managed."

Plus, unlike a true, every-person-for-themselves conflict, when done properly, both parties get what they want out of a negotiation. You get more money, and the other party receives quality work from an employee who isn't spending half the day tweaking her résumé.

## YOUR BOSS EXPECTS THIS

You wouldn't buy a car without haggling, because it's a cultural norm, Dr. Babcock said. The same should be true when it comes to your salary and benefits package.

"In our culture, there are things where people are always supposed to negotiate, like cars or houses," she said. "These are really clear-cut situations. Everything else is more uncertain, and knowing what's negotiable or not is more complicated."

(AAUW), adding that "H.R. costs for hiring new employees are high."

"Negotiating for your salary shouldn't change their decision," she said. However, this has other implications for women.

## NEGOTIATING IS GENDERED, SO PLAN ACCORDINGLY

Much of Dr. Babcock's research has focused on whether women are penalized when they ask for more. Unfortunately, the answer is yes.

"The style that a woman uses to negotiate can backfire and can create backlash, but using a cooperative style can get you what you want and help you avoid the backlash," she said, adding that women should be aware that negotiating forcefully can have repercussions. Is this unfair? Yes, but this is the sad reality women must contend with.

Here's the other kicker: Managing your approach is important regardless of your manager's gender.

"It's not just men to blame for this; women do this too," Dr. Babcock said. She cites research she published in Organizational Behavior and Human Decision in 2007, showing that both men and women penalized female employees when they initiated salary negotiations.

"Don't be timid, but use the right inflection and wording choices," Ms. Churches said, adding that paying close attention to the body language of the person you're negotiating with is important, too. If your boss's posture changes, tune in and adjust as needed.

Ms. Churches suggested adopting a collaborative approach, focusing on how you can help your company or organization grow. For example,

## DEFLECT ON YOUR SALARY HISTORY

Many employers ask about salary history and base your offer upon those past numbers. Try your best not to fall for it: There is no obligation—legal or otherwise—to disclose this information, so your first move should be to parry this question to see if your potential employer will throw out the first number.

Still, read the room: Sometimes you'll just have to cough it up.

When asked about your past compensation, she suggests a script like this one, which is available on the AAUW's online Salary Skill Builder Workshop: "This position is not the same as my last job, I'd like to discuss what my responsibilities would be here and then determine a fair salary for that job." Practice giving this response until it feels like second nature.

> 66
>
> *Focus on how you want to keep working with the organization and helping the company reach its goals.*

suggest additional responsibilities you'd like to take on or new skills you'd like to acquire. Focus on how you want to keep working with the organization and helping the company reach its goals.

What not to do: "Say I want X and 10 percent more a year after that, because I'm awesome and deserve it," Dr. Babcock said. "You'll be deemed as too aggressive."

## HAVE GOOD NUMBERS

If you do have to throw out the first number, you still have leveraging power, said Dr. Babcock.

"If you're well-calibrated, you actually can have an advantage throwing out a number first," she said. The trick here is knowing the market rate for your job.

"You can lose credibility if you're way too high," Dr. Babcock said. But being too low can set off alarm bells that you might lack experience or professionalism.

Finding that range is tricky, thanks in part to employers who discourage employees from talking to one another about their compensation.

However, thanks to the National Labor Relations Act, "that's illegal in nearly all private sector workplaces," according to Cynthia Estlund, a professor at the New York University School of Law. Certain types of managers, especially in the rail and airways industries, might be excluded from the labor relations law, so do a touch of research before asking around. But the majority of American workers are free to speak about their wages, Ms. Estlund said—and shouldn't be shy about it.

"There's this peculiar American aversion to talking about these things," she said. But research has shown that salary transparency leads to greater "wage compression," which Ms. Estlund said is another way of saying "equality."

"It means there is less difference between the bottom wages and the top," she said.

Sites like Glassdoor, PayScale and LinkedIn, as well as trade organizations, can also help you figure out where your salary should be. These sites, while not perfect, may be your best resource if your company actively bars employees from comparing notes on pay.

## FOLLOW A SCRIPT

The AAUW website offers tools that will help you write your own script, but a basic outline for a salary negotiation goes like this:

- Start with why you love your job and are excited to help the company grow.
- Highlight your successes and additional skills you've acquired.

- Suggest some ways you may be able to take on more responsibility.
- Finally, ask about how you can ensure your compensation matches your skills and responsibilities.

And don't forget to practice: Find a friend and ask them to poke holes in your résumé and push back in interview practice "so you're prepared for different scenarios," Ms. Churches said.

## YOU CAN'T ALWAYS GET WHAT YOU WANT

If you get what you want on the first try, congrats! But if your boss can't commit, you still have a few options.

"You can ask, 'How close do you think you can come to my number?'" Dr. Babcock said. This puts the decision back on them. If they still balk, ask how you can gain the skills needed to take you to the next level. Dr. Babcock said letting a boss in on your lofty aspirational goals can help them see you as an employee worth investing in.

Whatever happens, don't keep picking and picking at the no.

"Listen to your gut on how much you can go back and forth, then make some decisions," Ms. Churches said. "It takes two parties to negotiate," and if the other party isn't interested in keeping the dialogue going, you need to figure out how to move on. "You can do a Hail Mary and try one last time, or you can start looking elsewhere for employment."

Whatever you do, according to Dr. Babcock, remember: "There's no cost to being gracious, and if you're colleagues, you're in a long-term relationship with this person."

# How to Recognize Burnout Before You're Burned Out

BY KENNETH R. ROSEN

**IN TODAY'S ERA OF WORKPLACE BURNOUT,** achieving a simpatico work–life relationship seems practically out of reach. Being tired, ambivalent, stressed, cynical and overextended has become a normal part of a working professional life. The General Social Survey of 2016, a nationwide survey that since 1972 has tracked the attitudes and behaviors of American society, found that 50 percent of respondents are consistently exhausted because of work, compared with 18 percent two decades ago.

But occupational burnout goes beyond needing a simple vacation or a family retreat, and many experts, psychologists and institutions, including the Centers for Disease Control and Prevention (CDC), highlight long-term and unresolvable burnout as not a symptom but rather a major health concern.

It is difficult to identify burnout, which often feels like surrender or failure rather than what it really is: a chronic disease. But here are some warning signs—and how to fix the problem before it becomes serious.

## SIGNS OF BURNOUT TO WATCH FOR

The pioneering researcher behind the study of burnout since the 1970s, Christina Maslach, professor emerita of psychology at the University of California, Berkeley, conducted a study that concluded there are three major signs of workplace burnout.

**1.** Feeling emotionally drained and mentally unwell. Nausea. Being unable to sleep or constantly fighting sicknesses like head colds.

**2.** Feeling alienated by your colleagues and bosses, feeling constantly underappreciated, or feeling ostracized by them.

**3.** Feeling you are not personally achieving your best, or are regularly "phoning it in."

"There are a lot of things that can happen when people begin to have this problem at work," Dr. Maslach said. "There are things like absenteeism, turnover, but also things in terms of errors, not being careful about the work they're doing. We see a lot of difficulty with people getting along with each other—angry, aggressive."

In 1981, Dr. Maslach and her colleagues devised the Maslach Burnout Inventory. It is still used today to determine whether an employee is experiencing burnout that may be causing performance or personal issues.

"Stress phenomenon can take a toll in terms of physical health, which can then get tied into the absenteeism. There are a number of ways in which the quality of the work goes down as a result of burnout," she said.

If anyone complains about it, she said, they're automatically labeled a wimp.

"Quite honestly in America we glorify stress," Dr. Maslach said. "And that's another thing that leads people to be quiet and shut up about some of the stressors they're facing, because they don't want to be viewed [as] not doing their best."

### COMMON WORK STRESSORS TO AVOID

Challenges associated with new software, changing atmospheres or different processes

Unrealistic deadlines

Frequent scheduling conflicts or interruptions

Unpredictable schedules

Physical demands like exposure to weather or heavy lifting

Added responsibility beyond the initial scope of one's role while not being compensated for the supervision

Interpersonal demands such as interactions with colleagues or customers

# WAYS TO COMBAT BURNOUT AT WORK

If you're suffering from burnout at work, or if any of those symptoms sound familiar to you, there are a few things you can do now, before you get some time off to recover. (Although you should definitely consider some time off to recover, if you can.)

- Practice focused breathing, which can tap into your parasympathetic nervous system to help you reduce or manage stress.
- Take frequent breaks, preferably five-minute breaks for every 20 minutes spent on a single task, or sitting at your desk.
- Use ergonomic chairs and desks, like a sit-stand arrangement, or add a small plant in your office space.
- Find a trusted mentor at work with whom you can discuss and strategize other ways to deal with work-related issues.
- Engage in a hobby outside of work through which you can decompress, de-stress and dissociate from work. It doesn't have to be anything specific, but regular exercise or another fitness activity works wonders here, and has benefits beyond stress relief.

If you have the ability to work remotely, that's another great way to add stress-reducers to your life. Periodically working out of the office enables you to try working from a quiet and contemplative space in which creativity may grow. It could also allow for more time outdoors. But broadly speaking, Dr. Maslach said, it is the human connection that's most effective at combating burnout.

"What we found is that people's health, well-being, everything in life, is way better if you're connected with other people," she said. "That social network, that each of you have each other's back, that they're there for you and you're there for them, that's like money in the bank. That's a precious, precious resource."

Jason Lang is the team leader of Workplace Health Programs within the CDC. He says that aside from good diet, exercise and sleep, there's one surefire way to combat general malaise, job dissatisfaction, low morale and burnout.

"Laughter," he said. "Find some humor in daily life."

# How to Make the Most of Your Workday

BY PHYLLIS KORKKI

**DO YOU OFTEN FIND YOUR WORKDAY** spiraling out of control? You start each day with a plan to get so much done, but soon find yourself becoming distracted, focusing on low-priority tasks and, simply, procrastinating. So how can you regain control of your time? One-size-fits-all lists on how to be more productive don't work; we'll outline productivity techniques that can be adapted to your personality and working style.

## FOR THE PROCRASTINATOR

Accountability—whether it's to yourself or to another person—can be crucial to your productivity.

### Be Accountable

To combat procrastination, find an accountability partner. This can be a colleague or a manager, whose role is to receive regular progress reports on your project. The person you choose will have to take his or her role seriously, expressing disappointment if you have not achieved your goal, and appreciation if you have.

## THREE BASICS OF PRODUCTIVITY

**Trust the small increments.**
You can't expect to change years of working habits overnight. Small changes in how you work can gradually add up to big changes in productivity. Try one tip to start, and keep adding more as you find the strategies that work best for you.

**Be accountable.**
Whether it's weekly check-ins with a co-worker or setting your own deadlines and announcing them to others, having to answer to someone else can often force you to get the job done.

**Forgive yourself.**
You are human: Accept that you are sometimes going to slip up, become distracted and have a bad day. It's more important to move on than to dwell on your mistakes.

### Stay on Track

To-do lists work to keep you accountable because they help you stay on the path to getting your most important work done—if you use them effectively, that is.

Before you leave work for the day, make a list of five to eight goals that you would like to accomplish the following day, said Julie Morgenstern, a time management expert based in New York. On a separate list add any personal errands that need to be done that day—like booking a flight for a vacation or buying a birthday gift. That list should contain no more than two or three items.

Be realistic about what you can accomplish in a day of work, and resist the urge to make a to-do list for the whole week, which can leave you feeling stressed and overwhelmed. And make sure to make the items on your to-do list specific, realistic and simple. (And be careful not to become list-obsessed and spend more time writing lists than actually completing them.)

### List Keepers

Some people like to keep their lists on paper—making emphatic and satisfying checkmarks whenever they complete a task. Others prefer the computer route. If that's the case, many apps are available, including Todoist, Remember the Milk and the always popular Evernote.

### AT YOUR DESK

Where you work can be just as important as how you work.

### What Your Desk Says About You

Your physical workspace can have a big effect on productivity. It "can either energize you or deplete your energy," said Ms. Morgenstern, the time management expert.

"Every paper on your desk has a task associated with it, and that task is going to take time," Ms. Morgenstern said.

# FOR THE MULTITASKER

If you're trying to do three things at once, you're often accomplishing very little.

## A Biological Impossibility

We all have a limited amount of cognitive bandwidth—the number of thoughts and memories we can hold in our minds at any given time. Your ability to get things done depends on how well you can focus on one task at a time, whether it's for five minutes or an hour, and that ability decreases when you switch back and forth between tasks.

"Multitasking is not humanly possible," said Earl K. Miller, a neuroscience professor at the Picower Institute for Learning and Memory at the Massachusetts Institute of Technology.

## More Errors and Less Creativity

When you multitask, you tend to make more mistakes. When you toggle back and forth between tasks, the neural networks of your brain must backtrack to figure out where they left off and then reconfigure, Dr. Miller said. That extra activity causes you to slow down, and errors become more likely.

Trying to multitask also impedes creativity, Dr. Miller added. Truly innovative thinking arises when we allow our brains to follow a logical path of associated thoughts and ideas, and this is more likely when we can focus on a single mental pathway for an extended period.

Structure your day around strategies that will allow you to focus on one thing at a time. Here are some tips:

- **Remove temptation:** Actively resist the urge to check unrelated social media while you are working on a task. Some workers may need to go so far as to install anti-distraction programs like SelfControl, Freedom, StayFocusd and Anti-Social, which block access to the most addictive parts of the internet for specified periods.
- **Work on just one screen:** Put away your cell phone and turn off your second monitor.
- **Move:** If you find yourself losing focus—reading the same sentence over and over or if your mind continually wanders off topic—get up and briefly walk around.
- **Work in intervals:** Set a timer for 5 or 10 minutes and commit to focusing on your assignment for that amount of time. Then allow yourself a minute of distraction, as long as you get back on your task for another 5 or 10 minutes.

Remember: The tendency to become distracted is primal, so forgive yourself if you do.

Ask yourself: Are the piles on your desk the same ones that were there three weeks ago, or are they moving? As long as they're not stagnant, you're probably doing OK with some clutter, Ms. Morgenstern said.

In most cases, keep your desk clear except for the project you are tackling at the moment, along with the equipment you need to complete it. You should also create a space for an "in zone"—brand-new things that have just come in—and an "out zone" for things that are finished and need to be distributed.

Try to spend the last 10 minutes of your workday readying your desk for the next day, so you don't start your day with yesterday's mess.

## FOR COMPUTER USERS (EVERYONE)

As much as they speed up the pace of work, computers can slow things down, too.

### Know Your Computer

Not understanding the capabilities of your computer can be a serious hindrance to your productivity. Some people fear that asking for tech help will make them look incompetent, but in fact the opposite is true, according to research.

Ask for technology advice when you think a computer or online task is taking longer than it should. Make an effort to seek out the people who can fill in your knowledge gaps, while being respectful of their time and responsibilities.

### Take Control of Your Inbox

Email is like life: It is messy, imperfect, full of surprises and everybody handles it differently. There is no perfect email system. Experts may promote the value of techniques like "inbox zero," where you try to clear your inbox every day, but even if your inbox is empty, your work life—with all its unanswered questions, incomplete projects and challenging problems—will remain full. Embrace the daily challenge of keeping your work life under control by using email as your ally rather than your nemesis.

Here are a few techniques that can help make your email work for you:

**Set aside dedicated times every day to process email.** This could be a few times a day or five minutes every hour, Ms. Morgenstern, the time management expert, said. "Give email your undivided attention when you're working on it," she said.

**Divide email into groups.** As you scan your email, sort the messages into two groups: those requiring quick responses and those needing thoughtful ones. Try the "two-minute rule," as popularized by David Allen, author of "Getting Things Done." If you can dispense with an email in two minutes, do it now; if not, do it later at a scheduled time. If emails are going to require a few days of thought, buy yourself some time by acknowledging receipt that day and saying you will respond later. Make it a point to follow through.

**Try to identify the emails you are actively avoiding.** Often there is an emotional component to emails you avoid, Ms. Morgenstern said, because they involve saying no to someone or making a difficult decision. Instead of procrastinating on replying, you will likely save time by responding in person or on the phone, where your tone and personality will come through more readily, rather than trying to write the perfect diplomatic response in an email.

**Turn off notifications.** Some email experts advise checking email only two or three times a day, but in many work environments this is not realistic—an all-important message from the boss or a client may need a quick response. But almost anything can wait for 20 minutes. So, turn off your email notifications for 20 to 30 minutes when you need to focus on something else.

## FOR THOSE WHO POWER THROUGH

It's no surprise that the way you treat your body can affect the way your mind works.

### Move More

Working continuously and for long hours does not mean you're getting more done. Sometimes the best way to get something done is not to work on it for a while.

Sitting for long periods of time is just plain bad for you, but it's also bad for your ability to be productive. Standing up and moving around improves blood flow to the brain, which enhances cognition. Alan Hedge, an ergonomics professor at Cornell University, suggests that workers try a combination of sitting, standing and walking to keep altering their body position and give their minds a break from work.

### How to Make Desk Work More Productive

A timed combination of sitting, standing and walking can help you work at your best.

- Sit for 20 minutes and work.
- Stand for eight minutes and work.
- Stop working and take a walk for two minutes.
- Repeat.

### Take Long Breaks

Working a 10- to 12-hour day may earn you points with some bosses, but it's not great for creativity. Instead of powering through, consider intentionally taking a break from a large project for up to 10 hours. That will allow new ideas to marinate in your subconscious, causing your neurons to make new connections.

Sleep is one of the most effective ways to take a long break, so try not to give it short shrift. Research shows that sleep allows our brains to make new and unexpected connections, leading to insights and breakthroughs.

Learn to identify the signs of mental fatigue, like reading the same sentence over and over at websites or writing emails with no real goals or priorities in mind. Don't feel guilty about taking a break, or leaving for the day when you think that your brain needs time to recharge.

### Try a Nap

The midafternoon "post-lunch dip" can hit anyone, since your body naturally wants to go to sleep about seven hours after waking, and this is amplified by the effects of digestion. If it's possible to take a 20-minute "power nap" at work, by all means do so. To best increase your energy, it may be a good idea to drink a cup of coffee before your nap. Research has shown that this method likely works because the short power nap helps clear the brain of the sleep-inducing compound adenosine.

take quick, shallow breaths. This sends less oxygen to the brain, causing us to become even more stressed and to think less clearly. Counteract the effects of stress by breathing more efficiently.

Most people are vertical breathers, in that their shoulders move up when they inhale, according to

> " 
>
> ## Working with your body rather than against it, you will maximize the blood flow to your brain— and your mental capacity.

Caffeine, meanwhile, takes about 20 minutes to have its physiological effect—kicking in just as the napper is awakening.

If a nap is out of the question, train yourself to quickly recognize the signs of the post-lunch dip: drowsiness and an inability to concentrate. Then, get up and walk around, talk to a colleague at another desk or work on something less demanding of your brainpower until the sleepiness passes.

### Fight Stress

When we feel overwhelmed at work, our fight-or-flight response tends to come into play, leading us to

Belisa Vranich, a clinical psychologist and breath instructor. Many people also breathe from their upper chest, whereas the biggest part of the lungs is in the middle of the body.

Horizontal breathing may seem unnatural at first, but it is actually the way animals and small children breathe. Working with your body rather than against it, you will maximize the blood flow to your brain— and your mental capacity.

And pay attention to your posture, which allows you to breathe more fully, prevent chronic pain and think more clearly. Stress can force you into unnatural positions, negating the benefits of good posture.

# COMMON PRODUCTIVITY MYTHS

Here's the truth behind common misconceptions about working smart.

**MYTH** People who are good multitaskers get more done.

**FACT** Multitasking is an illusion. Research shows that people get more done if they concentrate on one task at a time. Switching frequently between tasks—or believing that you are actually doing more than one thing at once—will actually slow you down.

**MYTH** It's important to have zero emails in your inbox by the end of the day.

**FACT** The goal of "inbox zero" works for some people but not for others. The key to managing email is to designate specific times of the day for reading and responding to it, to differentiate between emails that can be handled quickly and those that require more time, and to learn how to use all of your email software's features (folders, filters and archives) in ways that work best for you.

**MYTH** It's best to stand while you work.

**FACT** It's better to change your position throughout the day, in a regular cycle of sitting, standing and moving around. Among other things, this variety helps bring more blood to your brain, improving your cognition and therefore your productivity.

**MYTH** The more hours you work, the more you get done.

**FACT** It is important to take breaks throughout the workday. Even a five-minute walk around the office can boost your mood with no impact on your ability to focus. Getting enough rest and sleep can serve you better than working longer hours. Walking away from your work for a longer period—overnight, over the weekend or on vacation—gives your ideas a chance to marinate in your subconscious mind, allowing for new bursts of productivity when you return.

# Why Your Brain Tricks You into Doing Less Important Tasks

BY TIM HERRERA

**HERE'S A LIST OF THINGS I DID BEFORE WRITING THIS STORY:** I filled out the documents to renew my passport; clipped my cat's nails; bought some household items; responded to a few Instagram DMs; and ate a snack because I was hungry.

Sound familiar?

Some of those tasks were relatively urgent—I need to get my passport in order soon, and those Instagram DMs were weighing on me. But none of those tasks were as important as writing this article. I knew I needed to get this done, but the call of those minor-yet-urgent tasks was too strong.

To all of my fellow procrastinators out there, I offer an explanation: Your brain is working against you, and it's because of a phenomenon called the *urgency effect*.

Our brains tend to prioritize immediate satisfaction over long-term rewards. But a 2018 study found that subjects were more likely to perform smaller but urgent tasks that had a deadline than they were to perform more important tasks without one. This was true even if the outcome of the smaller task was objectively worse than that of the larger one.

"Normatively speaking," the researchers wrote, "people may choose to perform urgent tasks with short completion windows, instead of important tasks with larger outcomes, because important tasks are more difficult and further away from goal completion, urgent tasks involve more immediate and certain payoffs, or people want to finish the urgent tasks first and then work on important tasks later."

In other words, even if we know a larger, less-urgent task is vastly more consequential, we will instinctively choose to do a smaller, urgent task anyway. Yet again, thanks for nothing, brain.

So what are we to do? To answer that, let's talk about boxes—specifically, one made famous by our 34th president, Dwight D. Eisenhower.

Picture a two-by-two square with four boxes. At the top of the square are two labels: urgent and not urgent. On the left are two other labels: important and not important.

Here's a visual.

On any given day, try to put every task you have to do into one of those four boxes. You'll quickly see that the things tied to approaching deadlines are quite often not the most important things you have on your plate. Accordingly, schedule time to finish them later or, if possible, delegate them.

Similarly, it's very likely you'll wind up with tasks that don't have a deadline and aren't important. Immediately and aggressively remove them from your to-do list.

Two crucial bits I'll leave you with:

**1.** If you're struggling to figure out whether something is important to you, spend some time looking inward to see if it's truly core to who you are and what your ambitions are.

**2.** Once you've mapped out all of your tasks, embrace the magic of micro-progress and slice them up into tiny goals to make them more manageable. (Read the story on micro-progress later in this chapter for tips.)

|  | URGENT | NOT URGENT |
|---|---|---|
| **IMPORTANT** |  |  |
| **NOT IMPORTANT** |  |  |

# Tips for Working from Home

BY KENNETH R. ROSEN

**THERE ARE MANY THINGS THAT CONTRIBUTE** to becoming a successful work-from-home employee. As more companies accommodate an increasing number of employees wishing to forgo the morning commute and office pantry footfall, remote work has become an increasingly easy and breathlessly viable option for many who seek it. Here are some tips to becoming a successful remote employee.

## GET DRESSED FOR THE DAY

Business attire is (obviously) not required, but act as though you will be interacting with colleagues in person. After all, you never know when they may want to video chat, and you don't want to beg off because you look unkempt or aren't wearing a shirt. (And don't forget to shower; you'd be surprised at how quickly that habit falls by the wayside.)

This also sets the tempo for the day and discourages the sleepy notion that, perhaps, just maybe, you can crawl back into bed for a nap around lunch—although, as we discussed in a previous section, if you need a nap to recharge, take it and don't feel guilty about it.

## DON'T SLEEP WHERE YOU WORK

Find a space away from your bedroom to work—and don't wake up to the blue hue of your smartphone and immediately start working. Set up shop in the kitchen or another space in your home; the idea is just to have a place that is for work that is separate from your resting space.

Worst case, toss your laptop in your bag, grab a pair of headphones and head to a local coffee shop that has Wi-Fi or even a quiet spot at your local library to set up shop and get things done. Just be courteous if you plan to make a public space your office—be sure that coffee shop is OK with people working there for long hours, and make your all-day presence at one of their tables worthwhile by buying food and drinks.

## STAY CONNECTED

Before divorcing completely from the office, check with your corporate IT department and your manager to see if you are equipped with the programs and applications necessary to work remotely.

Security first: If you connect to your company's internal systems or email through a virtual private network or other secure tunnel, make sure you've tested it and that it functions from where you plan to work. Also, have a backup plan in the event your internet connection experiences disruptions. (Like that coffee shop.)

## COMMUNICATE OFTEN

The ability to communicate quickly and reliably is the most priceless attribute a remote employee needs to succeed. Update your manager or boss frequently. Most offices use some group chat service,

## MANAGE YOUR TIME

Follow the S.M.A.R.T. goal approach: Make sure your to-do list for the day includes tasks that are specific, measurable, achievable, realistic and time-bound.

If you find yourself struggling to stay focused, one strategy is to try the Pomodoro productivity technique: Work for a specific interval of time—say, 25 minutes—then take a five-minute break. Rinse and repeat.

*For more information on this, see the section of this chapter called "How to Make the Most of Your Workday."*

like Slack, to communicate with each other during the day, and tools like Google Hangouts or Skype for video calls and meetings. Make sure they're installed and you know how to use them, and make your presence known to your colleagues (especially your boss) when you are available and working.

Find out which of those platforms are the most convenient for the people with whom you frequently communicate, and agree that you'll prioritize that avenue for most of your communications.

## PLAN AGAINST DISTRACTIONS

Block out disturbances. Set (and enforce) boundaries if you're working at home by explaining to family members or children that your work area is off limits, and they should avoid interrupting unless it's important. Set aside time and breaks to spend with them so they don't feel entitled to your working time.

said Kevin Purdy, a staff writer at The Wirecutter who has worked from home full time for roughly a decade. "It helps you feel like you have a regular schedule, gives you some outside inspiration, and if nothing else, it enforces the Wear Pants rule at least once or twice a week."

> " 
> **Set aside time and breaks to spend [with family members or children] so they don't feel entitled to your working time.**

The same goes for social media and the unlimited distractions waiting for you online. Apps available for Google Chrome, such as StayFocusd, allot a specific amount of time per day on select websites (like Facebook or Twitter) before rendering those sites inaccessible for the remainder of the day. Other web apps, like Strict Workflow and TomatoTimer, act as timers to help you stay focused when you need to.

## GET OUT

One of the blessings of working remotely is the opportunity to live a more active lifestyle instead of being deskbound, so make activity a habit. Otherwise you'll fall into the inertia of sitting at your desk all day and never leaving the house at night—not to mention the inherent loneliness that can come with working remotely.

"Have a regularly scheduled social meeting: pre-work coffee, lunch with a friend or group of friends,"

## WHEN YOU LOG OFF, ACTUALLY LOG OFF

Separating your technology from the place where you come to recharge and disconnect at the end of the day is invaluable to the discipline needed for working remotely. When you log off for the day, log off. Close your work chat programs and emails and consider yourself "out for the day" and "home now."

Trying to mix work and free time runs the danger of never quite powering down or shutting off, and can lead to burnout and depression from feeling like you're always on and available. Set your boundaries, and aggressively enforce them.

# What is the worst job interview you've ever had?

**Lauren McGoodwin** had a mortifying misstep when interviewing for her first job: She spelled "experience" wrong on her résumé. "The hiring manager noticed it and started to endlessly circle it with a red pen. She interrupted me to tell me, 'Oh boy! You spelled "experience" wrong. You must struggle with being detail-oriented. Tell me why we should hire you if you can't spell "experience" or at least can't be trusted to check your work before you turn it in.'" Ms. McGoodwin didn't get that job, but she's made crafting the perfect résumé into her life's work: She's founder and CEO of Career Contessa, a career development platform that provides resources to help women build successful careers, and she is also the creator of The Salary Project and host of "The Femails" podcast.

Investor and author **Patrick McGinnis**—who coined the acronym "FOMO" (Fear of Missing Out) while at Harvard Business School—was busy trying to get a summer job with an elite consulting firm. "I'd never been good at case study interviews, and I'm going through one about metal production of hairspray cans, and I couldn't get the answer. I was throwing out anything. The guy stops me and is like, 'Paddy, for f***'s sake, let me give you the answer.' It was shocking. I never interviewed with another consulting firm after that day." But after the humiliation faded, Mr. McGinnis found the experience liberating. "This was clearly not the path for me. The experience freed me from trying to do the default."

**Kashif Naqshbandi's** job interview gaffe came in the form of the nightclub stamp from the evening before, which he noticed when he reached out to greet his interviewer. "I could tell they noticed the crude smudge on the back of my hand, but they didn't address it, which made matters even worse," he said. "I felt I had to compensate for my indiscretion and probably came across as too serious or straitlaced."

In retrospect, he notes, he should have just addressed it. "It shows honesty and willingness to discuss difficult or sensitive subjects. You also shouldn't be embarrassed about who you are, and definitely shouldn't let it impact you professionally." Now Mr. Naqshbandi is chief marketing officer at Frank Recruitment Group, a global niche technology recruitment agency.

# Micro-progress and the Magic of Just Getting Started

## BY TIM HERRERA

**I'VE NEVER BEEN GREAT WITH DEADLINES.**

It's a flaw I'm keenly aware of, and one I actively try to counter. But despite my best efforts, it's forever lingering in the background, an insatiable little gremlin that devours my productivity. It is definitely one of my "things." (See pages 34–35 for more on that.)

Yet of the countless articles, books and so-called lifehacks about productivity I've read (or written!), the only "trick" that has ever truly and consistently worked is both the simplest and the most difficult to master: just getting started.

Enter *micro-progress*.

Pardon the gimmicky phrase, but the idea goes like this: For any task you have to complete, break it down into the smallest possible units of progress and attack them one at a time.

Let's say you're an editor with a weekly newsletter to write. Rather than approach that task as "Write Monday's newsletter," break down the very first steps you have to take and keep slicing them up into tiny, easily achievable *micro-goals*, then celebrate each achievement:

**Step 1:** Open a Google Doc.
**Step 2:** Name that Google Doc.
**Step 3:** Write a single sentence.

This is an idea that has been given many names—the five-minute rule, the two-minute rule and the one-minute rule, to name a few—but these techniques thinking into this frame—I've started being productive, so I'm going to keep being productive—you achieve those micro-goals at what feels like an exponentially increasing rate without even realizing it.

And it's not just gimmicky phrases and so-called lifehacking: Studies have shown that you can trick your brain into increasing dopamine levels by setting and achieving, you guessed it, micro-goals.

Going even further, success begets success. In a 2011 Harvard Business Review article, researchers reported finding that "ordinary, incremental progress can increase people's engagement in the work and their happiness during the workday." That means that once you start that PowerPoint you're

> " 
>
> ### For any task you have to complete, break it down into the smallest possible units of progress and attack them one at a time.

only get you going on a task. My favorite expansion of this concept is in this story by the author James Clear.

In it, he uses Newton's laws of motion as analogies for productivity. Rule Number One: "Objects in motion tend to stay in motion. Find a way to get started in less than two minutes."

What's so striking about applying this law of motion to productivity is that once you shift your dreading, even if all you've done is give it a name, that micro-progress can continue to build on itself until you've finally finished that last slide.

But all of that success has to begin somewhere. So go get started on that one thing you've been putting off.

# Take Naps at Work. Apologize to No One.

## BY TIM HERRERA

**I AM AGGRESSIVELY, UNAPOLOGETICALLY** a fan of sleeping at work. I have no shame or uncertainty about doing it, and I couldn't feel better about it. My productivity reflects it, too.

Sleeping on the job is one of those workplace taboos—like leaving your desk for lunch or taking an afternoon walk—that we're taught to look down on. If someone naps at two p.m. while the rest of us furiously write memos and respond to emails, surely it must mean he's slacking off. Or so the assumption goes.

Restfulness and recharging can take a back seat to the perception and appearance of productivity. It's easier to stay on a virtual hamster wheel of activity by immediately responding to every email than it is to measure aggregate productivity over a greater period of time. But a growing field of occupational and psychological research is building the case for restfulness in pursuit of greater productivity.

"Companies are suffering from tremendous productivity problems because people are stressed out" and not recovering from the workday, said Josh Bersin, principal and founder of Bersin by Deloitte. "They're beginning to realize that this is their problem, and they can't just say to people, 'Here's a work-life balance course, go teach yourself how to manage your inbox,'" Mr. Bersin said. "It's way more complicated than that."

To be sure, the ability to nap at work is far from widespread, experts said. Few among us have the luxury of being able to step away for a half-hour snoozefest. But lunch hours and coffee breaks can be great times to duck out, and your increased productivity and alertness will be all the evidence you need to make your case to inquiring bosses.

said Sara Mednick, a co-author of the study and associate professor of psychology at the University of California, Riverside.

Dr. Mednick, a sleep researcher and the author of "Take a Nap! Change Your Life," said daytime napping can have many of the benefits of overnight sleep, and different types of naps offer specific benefits.

For example, Dr. Mednick said a 20- to 60-minute nap might help with memorization and learning

> **The Japanese have a word for strategically sleeping on the job: "inemuri," roughly translated to "sleeping while present."**

In an ideal world, we'd all solve this problem by unplugging early and getting a good night's sleep. But the next best thing is stealing away for a quick power nap when you're dragging after lunch.

The Japanese even have a word for strategically sleeping on the job: "inemuri," roughly translated to "sleeping while present." Now is a good moment to show this story to your boss.

In a study published in Nature Neuroscience, researchers tested subjects on their perceptual performance four times throughout the day. Performance deteriorated with each test, but subjects who took a 30-minute nap between tests stopped the deterioration in performance, and those who took a 60-minute nap even reversed it.

"Naps had the same magnitude of benefits as full nights of sleep if they had a specific quality of nap,"

specific bits of information. It's just long enough to enter stage-two sleep, or non-rapid eye movement (REM) sleep.

After 60 minutes, you start getting into REM sleep, most often associated with that deep, dreaming state we all enjoy at night. REM sleep can improve creativity, perceptual processing and highly associative thinking, which allows you to make connections between disparate ideas, Dr. Mednick said. Beyond that, your best bet is a 90-minute nap, which will give you a full sleep cycle.

Any nap, however, can help with alertness and perception and cut through the general fog that creeps in during the day, experts said.

So how did we even arrive at this point where aptitude is inextricably tied to working long, concentrated hours? Blame technology, but think broader than smartphones and laptops; the real issue is that tech has enabled us to be available at all times.

"We went through a period where people were in denial and business leaders were ignoring it," Mr. Bersin said. "They were assuming that if we give people more tools, more emails, more Slack, more chatter, and we'll just assume they can figure out how to deal with it all. And I think they've woken up to the fact that this is a big problem, and it is affecting productivity, engagement, health, safety, wellness and all sorts of things."

It isn't just office workers who can benefit from an afternoon siesta. A 2015 study published in Current Biology looked at the sleeping habits of three hunter-gatherer preindustrial societies in Tanzania, Namibia and Bolivia.

"They're active in the morning, then they get in the shade under the trees and have a sort of quiet time, but they're not generally napping," said Jerome Siegel, professor of psychiatry and bio-behavioral sciences, and director of the UCLA Center for Sleep Research, a co-author of the study. "Then they do some work and go to sleep, and they sleep through the night."

Still, Mr. Siegel said the only genuine way to solve daytime sleepiness and fatigue starts the night before with a solid night's sleep. The real Holy Grail of restfulness is a regular sleep schedule with ideally seven or eight hours of sleep each night, which experts say is optimal.

"Daytime napping certainly does increase alertness," Mr. Siegel said. "But it's not as simple as going to the gas station and filling the tank."

He also advises avoiding caffeine late in the day and waking around the same time every morning, even if you can't get to sleep at the same time every night. This helps acclimate your body to your regular wake-up time, regardless of how much sleep you got the night before.

## A QUICK GUIDE TO THE PERFECT NAP

Find a quiet, unoccupied space where you won't be disturbed.

Try to make your area as dim as possible (or invest in a sleep mask you can keep in the office). Earplugs might help, too.

Aim for around 20 minutes. Any longer than that and you're likely to wake up with sleep inertia, which will leave you even groggier than before.

# Ghosts, Sea Gulls and Incompetents: How to Deal with Bad Bosses

BY TIM HERRERA

**ABOUT HALF OF AMERICAN WORKERS HAVE LEFT A JOB** to get away from a terrible boss. Half! That is crazy! And only 21 percent of workers think their performance "is managed in a way that motivates them to do outstanding work," according to Gallup's 2017 State of the American Workplace.

A full-time worker will spend more than 2,000 hours at work every year, so having a bad boss has an immense impact on our overall well-being and happiness. At its worst, it can even lead to symptoms akin to PTSD.

But having a bad manager doesn't always mean you should up and quit. (Unless it does—more on that later.) There are many reasons we might have a bad relationship with our manager, but often it comes down to poor communication, or a lack of it, according to Mary Abbajay, author of "Managing Up: How to Move up, Win at Work and Succeed with Any Type of Boss."

"You have to think about how you like to communicate," she said, then "understand how your boss likes to communicate and assess the gap between and figure out what you can do differently."

Cultivating better communication with your boss is easier than it sounds, and Ms. Abbajay has a simple script you can follow to figure it out. Ask your boss to coffee, and ask her these three questions:

**1**

What are your preferences in terms of how you like to communicate?

**2**

What are your priorities?

**3**

What are your pet peeves?

That's it! These questions are designed to get at the core of the manager-employee relationship, and having an open, honest conversation around them can save an ailing relationship or bolster a solid one.

However: "If the well is poisoned, the well is poisoned," Ms. Abbajay said. Signs to watch out for include spending more time thinking about how to deal with your boss than actually working, dreading going to work every day and feeling physically or mentally exhausted or sick. "If you've tried everything you could think of," she added, "you owe it to yourself to leave."

She added, "Work with the boss you have, not the boss you want."

Managers come in many different flavors, Ms. Abbajay said, naming a few: You might have a ghost boss (a manager who rarely communicates with you and is seemingly never around); a sea gull (bosses who she said swoop and poop or swoop and scoop, meaning they "divebomb into a project" and

our perception of his or her behavior, and not necessarily the reality of how he or she is acting. This is called the fundamental attribution error, a cognitive bias that leads us to attribute behavior we don't like to other people's characters, rather than to circumstances or outside factors.

"Understand that whenever we see behavior in someone that isn't what we want, we tend to make

> " 
> The thing to keep in mind...is that often the relationship we have with our boss is based on our perception of his or her behavior, and not necessarily the reality of how he or she is acting.

leave a mess behind, "or they dive into it and take it away from you"); or a simple incompetent ("the Michael Scotts of the world"). And, of course, most managers are a combination of different styles.

The thing to keep in mind, however, is that often the relationship we have with our boss is based on

up a story about why they're doing these things," Ms. Abbajay said. We think, "They're ghosting me, so they don't care about me. That may be true, but another story could be they're really busy, or they just trust you."

# Why You Should Take Time to Mourn During Career Transitions

BY KIMBERLY LAWSON

**ON MY LAST DAY IN THE NEWSROOM** at a North Carolina alt-weekly, I found myself choking back tears. For the first time in almost a decade, my desk was completely clean. All of my old reporter notebooks, past newspaper editions and sticky notes with scribbled writing on them were in the trash.

At the time, I didn't think I'd be sad to leave—I chose to quit, after all. But, to my surprise, I did feel as if I'd lost something important, and I felt that way for months, mostly because I never stopped to consider why.

But feelings of grief are common when you leave a workplace you love, said Kim Scott, author of "Radical Candor."

"Even if you're moving on to something that you really want to do and it's the right decision, change is really hard," Ms. Scott said.

She said it's important to take time, both before you leave a job and after you've started a new one, to process these transitions. Dealing with bouts of grief instead of ignoring them can help you better navigate the complex emotions of leaving a job you love and starting fresh somewhere new.

Why do we feel sad when we move on from a job?

For many Americans, identity is tied to work. According to a 2014 Gallup Poll, more than half of workers in the United States define themselves based on their job, and have been doing so consistently since 1989.

But it's important to figure out whether you identify with your professional occupation or with the organization you work at.

"If you're a technology person and you leave Google, you're still a technology person," said Amy Wrzesniewski, a professor at the Yale School of Man-

Compounding those feelings is the sheer amount of time we spend at our jobs. In 2015, Americans worked an average of 46.8 weeks per year, compared with 43 weeks in 1980, according to an analysis of Labor Department data from the Pew Research Center. (Not to mention the time we spend on ambient work, like dashing off a quick email from your smartphone at nine p.m.)

There's also the realization of who we're leaving behind. Colleagues can serve as "pseudo-family," said Dr. Lisa Orbé-Austin, a psychologist in New

> **66**
>
> *Dealing with bouts of grief instead of ignoring them can help you better navigate the complex emotions of leaving a job you love and starting fresh somewhere new.*

agement. But if you identify much more with being an employee of Google, she said, "You're in a different boat than someone who sees themselves as a programmer who creates things and could do that anywhere."

In either case, what informs that connection to work is the human need for a sense of belonging, said Beth Humberd, an assistant professor of management at the University of Massachusetts, Lowell.

"We want to be a part of something, and we want to be seen as needed in an area," she said.

Dr. Wrzesniewski added that for many people, what they do professionally is symbolic of other things. "It's symbolic of the things you care about," she said. "It's symbolic of your talents. It's symbolic of your offering to the world."

York, and you might not recognize that until after you've moved on.

"While we work, our lives happen—births, deaths, breakups—and our colleagues are often there to mourn with us and to celebrate the new transitions in our personal lives," Dr. Orbé-Austin said. "We share our lives in the workplace often in very intimate ways. All of these things provide deepening connections, support, and built-in social opportunities that we sometimes take for granted."

So, how can I prepare myself?

Remember that grief might come, perhaps unexpectedly.

"Part of it is just not getting caught off-guard by the fact that it's normal to have those feelings," said

Ms. Scott, who used to work at Google in sales and operations. On her last day at the company, Ms. Scott said she started "sobbing" when a member of human resources came to take her identification badge.

"He was shocked, and I was shocked," she said.

Lynn Berger, a New York-based career coach, suggested taking time to ponder what work means to you and what you get out of it. Do you go to work solely for practical reasons (e.g., financial security)?

Molly Barker, the founder of the nonprofit Girls on the Run in Charlotte, N.C., said she was "very intentional" about preparing for her departure as she retired in 2013 after 17 years at the organization. It took her about three years to figure out how to exit in a positive way, and she talked through everything with a small group of people she trusted.

Another concrete step to take when leaving, Dr. Orbé-Austin said, is to have a succession plan.

> **66**
>
> **When you understand what it is about your job that fulfills you the most, you may be able to prepare yourself if that's lacking in your new position.**

Do you enjoy being challenged at your job? Is work the primary place you socialize with other people? When you understand what it is about your job that fulfills you the most, Ms. Berger said, you may be able to prepare yourself if that's lacking in your new position.

"The more time you prepare yourself for this, the easier it's going to be," she added.

This can mean creating a list of all your responsibilities, or putting together a list of important contacts, or something else altogether. This can help your successor, but it's also a way for you to reflect on everything you've done at that job.

"It's almost like processing your experience there very proactively in a very classy way," Dr. Orbé-Austin said.

# I'VE STARTED MY NEW JOB—
# BUT I'M STILL MOURNING MY OLD WORK LIFE

That's totally normal, and everyone processes career transitions differently. Some people might not be fazed when they leave behind a role they considered profound. Others might feel sadness or a sense of loss they don't understand. Anger, frustration and anxiety can also crop up from time to time. Further still, you might feel a confusing mix of all of those emotions—or none of them at all.

Shana Wilson Anderson, 42, is a senior manager of training and delivery at Capital One, but in March, she said goodbye to the company she spent 18 years at. She started at T-Mobile in Georgia as a customer service representative and made her way up to senior manager of operations.

Ms. Anderson said she still hasn't gotten over the grief of leaving, adding that on her last day, there wasn't "a dry eye" in the call center. "I am an organized person, a planner, a strategic thinker," she said. "What I did not plan for was how I would really feel when I left the company."

This is what grief looks like, Dr. Orbé-Austin said, and it's OK to allow yourself to feel it. But if you're having trouble letting go, it can be helpful to identify exactly what you miss about the old workplace so you can address that loss head-on.

"If it's the relationships, you can plan regular happy hours so that you can stay in touch," Dr. Orbé-Austin said. "If it's identity loss, then you can work on formulating a new sense of identity that helps repair the loss and connecting more thoughtfully to your new work identity or your new workplace."

Work is more than simply what we do, she added.

"It's really important to value the complexity of what goes on at work. It isn't this experience where you just execute tasks," Dr. Orbé-Austin said. "There are really complex, dynamic growth experiences that are occurring, and when you experience loss, you're acknowledging the full breadth of all you experienced at that workplace."

# How to Perfect the Art of a Work Uniform

BY BRIAN MOYLAN

**MY CLOSET LOOKS EXACTLY LIKE DONALD DUCK'S:** two dozen identical shirts all in a row.

About three years ago I decided to start wearing a uniform to the office, so I went to J.Crew and ordered three of the same suit in the same fabric and a score of white oxford shirts with button-down collars. My uniform, I thought, would free me from the daily anxiety of standing in front of my closet wondering, "Does this match?" or "Am I wearing this sweater too often?"

At first, I had just swapped one anxiety for another: Would people think I was lazy or boring for wearing a uniform? But as I eased into my new uniform lifestyle, I started to feel better at work because I knew I would look good and I would be dressed perfectly for almost any occasion. Simply put, the decision to go all uniform all the time is one of the best I've ever made. I had joined the ranks of very successful people who dress the same every day—Steve Jobs, Mark Zuckerberg—and I appreciated that I could so easily communicate who I am.

"The whole idea of uniformity and adopting a uniform for yourself, it keeps things very simple," said the fashion designer Thom Browne, who wears one of his signature "shrunken" gray suits every day.

"I think there's something refreshing when you see someone who has a true sense of their own style," Mr. Browne said, joking that his uniform is so consistent he could probably get dressed in the dark.

"There is a real confidence in being able to project that image," he added. "I hope that's what people see as well."

Research supports that correlation between self-confidence and the way we present ourselves. In one study from 2012, people were given a coat

person. It's kind of like Dumbo's magic feather, but hopefully covering a lot more skin.

Dr. Galinsky added that when a person starts to embody that persona in the office, co-workers will recognize it, reinforcing that persona in the wearer's mind. This creates an endless feedback loop between how a person wants to be perceived and how they are perceived.

Basically, this is the psychological justification for the "dress for the job you want, not the job you

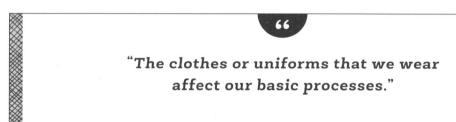

## "The clothes or uniforms that we wear affect our basic processes."

and told it was either a doctor's coat or an artist's smock. Researchers found that the subjects paid more attention to certain tasks when they thought they were wearing a doctor's coat, but that there was no improvement in performance when they thought it was an artist's smock.

Dr. Adam Galinsky, who ran the study and is a psychologist and professor at Columbia Business School, calls this "enclothed cognition." When we wear certain clothes, particularly uniforms, we take on the characteristics associated with those uniforms.

"The clothes or uniforms that we wear affect our basic processes," Dr. Galinsky said.

For this to work, a person has to understand the symbolism associated with a given outfit. So, if a person begins to conflate their work uniform with a certain persona, they will start to embody that

have" speech your mother gave you when she bought you your first interview suit after you graduated from college.

So what should shoppers do when looking to start a uniform?

"The key question you're asking is, What behavior do we want to produce and what impression do we want to portray?" Dr. Galinsky said. "You work backward from that into that uniform."

Dawnn Karen, a fashion psychologist who teaches at the Fashion Institute of Technology, added that people should look to dress appropriately for their specific office.

"You don't want to be in a tutu when everyone else is wearing a suit," she said, adding that it goes both ways. For those at a tech firm, a few pairs of the same jeans and two dozen of the most comfortable

T-shirts and hoodies are going to get you a lot further than a closet full of stuffy suits.

Rather than creating a uniform, Lauren A. Rothman, a stylist who lives in Washington and wrote the book "Style Bible: What to Wear to Work," practices "capsule dressing" with her clients, which is curating a small set of clothing that can be mixed or matched together. She suggests four capsules, one for each season. She added that people generally wore only about 25 percent of what was in their closets, so start by finding that 25 percent and replicating it.

"The problem with variety is that it is unpredictable and can be unsuccessful," Ms. Rothman said. "A uniform does communicate who you are. It is great if you have consistent messaging every day about who you are, and what you wear will show that."

When you are buying a uniform, take comfort into account, but also body type, physique and what will make you look and feel good, Ms. Rothman said. And while budget is always a consideration, it does not mean a solid collection can't be found inexpensively.

"A great capsule can be created at Kohl's and Bonobos as it can at Neiman's or Nordstorm," Ms. Rothman said.

Mr. Browne suggests people stick with high-quality goods, things that will last a long time through repeated wearing, and to consider tailoring when possible.

## EXPRESS YOURSELF

Wearing the same outfit every day doesn't mean you can't embellish. Just remember that when you're working with a uniform, a little bit goes a long way.

A splash of jewelry, a subtle wristwatch or a pair of shoes that scream out for attention can be all you need to up your style game.

And don't forget you can still customize the details. Dawnn Karen got a client out of her all-black clothing rut by incorporating more jewelry into the client's everyday attire. For men, consider a rotation of lapel pins, colorful socks and shiny shoes to mix things up.

One admittedly clichéd sentiment worth remembering: Less is more. That is certainly a philosophy that Donald Duck, my uniform bête-noire, subscribes to as well.

After all, he never even bothered to buy pants.

# SO WHAT IS "BUSINESS CASUAL," ANYWAY?

By Lizz Schumer

That ambiguous dress code can mean many things to many people in many different contexts. There aren't any hard-and-fast rules, so here are a few things to keep in mind next time you're asking yourself what to wear.

## Stock your wardrobe with flexible, mix-and-match options

If you are dressing for a new job, resist the urge to go on a shopping spree right away, and stock up on a few relatively neutral outfits for your first week. Take that time to watch what your new co-workers wear and follow their lead.

Alison Gary, a stylist and founder of the Washington-based style website Wardrobe Oxygen, specializes in capsule wardrobes, and she likes hitting the sales rack to find a few things you can wear regularly.

"There's no need to have 30 pairs of pants in your wardrobe, if you can find a good pair," she says. "No one is going to know if you're wearing the same pair of pants two or three times in a week if you're styling them in different ways." The office, she says, "is not the runway."

Start with a classic blazer, a pair of well-fitting pants, a blouse or button-down shirt and a sweater that can all mix and match.

## East vs. West: Geography, and industry, matters

When deciding what is office-appropriate, the location of your office and your industry are important. In general, Silicon Valley tech, nonprofit and start-up culture skew more casual than New York City finance and business, which are different from what Nashville lawyers might wear. Look around for clues, and when in doubt, ask.

"I know that being in D.C., our version of business casual is drastically different from Silicon Valley business casual," Ms. Gary says. "Theirs is, 'Don't wear flip-flops,' where ours is, 'Don't wear denim except on Friday.'"

Dress for your audience, too. Your attire "should say, 'I care.' I think that that's really what it boils down to," says Diane Gottsman, an etiquette expert, author and founder of the Protocol School of Texas. "Having respect for the people that you're with, and having respect for yourself, as well."

Bottom line? You want your attire to inspire confidence in your colleagues, managers and clients.

"People make judgments based on what they see, and that perception becomes their version of the truth," Ms. Gottsman says. "Dressing in a professional manner shows you pay attention to detail and take pride in yourself, which also translates into your work."

# 2

# Nest

## DECORATING · CLEANING AND MAINTENANCE · ENTERTAINING

**OUR HOME SHOULD BE** a place of refuge, relaxation and rest. But after work, visits to the gym, running errands, socializing and everything else your days are filled with, your home often becomes an afterthought.

It's time to reclaim your house, apartment or wherever you live and make it into the nest it should truly be.

Let us help you make the work of keeping a home simpler, and give you more time for the relaxing, resting and binge-watching we'd all rather be doing.

**READ MORE TO LEARN:**

- How changing a light bulb can change the whole feel of a room

- The best way to brighten your whites

- Tips for making cleaning your home simpler (and maybe even fun)

- Why you should store your important documents in your linen closet

- And how to keep your house running like new, year round

# A Beginner's Guide to Decorating Your Home

BY MICHELLE HIGGINS

**MAYBE YOU'RE JUST STARTING OUT,** with a new job and a new apartment—or maybe you're not. Either way, like many people, you may be on a tight budget, with little left over for decorating.

Here are tips from several design professionals on how to make your place look sophisticated and thoughtful without spending a fortune.

## INVEST IN THE ESSENTIALS

"I always tell people who are decorating their first apartments that it is important to spend money on the bigger-ticket items, like sofas, beds and dining tables," said the interior designer Sheila Bridges. "You can always accessorize with inexpensive things like toss pillows, bedding and lighting to pull everything together." Investment pieces—like that little black dress or the perfect-fitting blazer in your wardrobe—will act as a foundation you can build on.

## MAKE SURE YOU CAN TAKE IT WITH YOU

If this is your first place, "it is likely that you will move in the next few years," Ms. Bridges said. A well-made sofa or bed can go with you, but you're not going to take the wallpaper. Likewise, it doesn't make sense to splurge on custom curtains that won't fit the windows in your next home.

Art, on the other hand, "will make a huge impact on your space and can be brought with you from apartment to apartment," said Megan Opel, an interior designer at Megan Opel Interiors, an online design service. "I advise splurging on original paintings from your favorite artists, because nothing will make a space feel more like you than personally curated art."

But it doesn't have to cost a lot. "Custom framing can take any hand-me-down or thrift-store find from trash to treasure," said Kimberly Winthrop, a senior designer at Kimberly Winthrop Interiors, who recommends Framebridge.com for "affordable and quick custom framing."

## UPGRADE YOUR LIGHTING

It might not occur to most people to swap out existing light fixtures. But as Ms. Winthrop pointed out: "Changing the lighting is much easier than you think and can make a big impact. It is also very easy to swap back out when the time comes for you to move out."

## PASS ON PRICEY ACCESSORIES

Don't blow your budget on throw pillows, blankets or towels—or anything else that you know you'll have to replace on a regular basis. Apart from the wear-and-tear aspect, Ms. Winthrop said, "our taste in home

### GO VINTAGE

Sites like Chairish, Craigslist and eBay are a great source of reasonably priced antique and vintage coffee tables, dining tables and chairs, said Ms. Opel of Megan Opel Interiors, who found an expandable Henredon table and six cane chairs on Craigslist for $500. The search might take a little more time and effort—Ms. Opel looked for months—but "the payoff is big when you find quality items at a steal," she said.

And as Maxwell Ryan, the founder of Apartment Therapy, noted, it's not just about saving money: Vintage pieces add character to your space. Mr. Ryan said he recently visited the home of a friend that was decorated—and not cheaply—with all new furnishings, and "the whole house felt so impersonal and so lifeless, even though it was pretty." If you want a home that's warm, cozy and inviting, he said, a good rule of thumb is to "always have at least 25 percent used, vintage or hand-me-down furniture."

décor can sometimes change as often as our taste or trends in fashion." And changing small things like these is an easy way to refresh your space.

## DON'T FORGET THE KITCHEN

You can do a lot with everyday objects to jazz up the kitchen, said Maxwell Ryan, who likes to pick up beautifully packaged foods like cookies from Lazzaroni Amaretti that come in bright, distinctive tins he can leave on display. A couple of strategically placed bottles of wine, a basket of fruit or a good

## ABOVE ALL, RESTRAIN YOURSELF

"In the excitement of moving into their first apartment, people are all too often in a rush to do everything all at once and fill the space immediately with one exhilarating shopping trip," said Sir Terence Conran, the British design guru, retailer and restaurateur. "I have always thought it much better to live with your home first and understand the space before gradually furnishing it and adding color."

He continued: "Obviously you need the basics in place to live there, but by buying one or two pieces

> "I have always thought it much better to live with your home first and understand the space before gradually furnishing it and adding color."

cutting board, he said, will add color and warmth to any counter as well. "I also like to save corks and put them in a bowl."

When it comes to glasses and dinnerware, Mr. Ryan advised keeping it simple. "I'm a big fan of stemless wineglasses," he said, because they can be used for all kinds of drinks, so you don't have to waste space or money on different types of glasses. His suggestion for a good splurge? Buy three quality knives and a few really good pots and pans that you can keep forever. If that's not an option, you can pick up most kitchen basics at a restaurant supply store for a couple hundred dollars.

at a time, I think you have a better chance of creating a first apartment that works well and reflects your personality, which can only make you happier."

Investing in one thing at a time will also allow you to save up for higher-quality pieces. Start with essential furnishings for where you will sleep, eat and sit; side tables, credenzas and curtains can all come later.

Of course, if you are too strapped to invest in anything major at the moment, there is another option: "Buy cheap, modest furniture (Ikea is excellent) that fits the space you are living in and your style of life," Mr. Conran suggested. "As you move up the property ladder and get a bit more money in your pocket, then you can think about furniture that will last a lifetime."

# Eight Cheap, Landlord-Friendly Ways to Upgrade Your Rental

### BY KRISTIN WONG

**WHEN YOU RENT YOUR HOUSE OR APARTMENT,** your home renovation options are limited. You probably don't want to spend thousands upgrading your kitchen, for example, only to move out in a few years—and risk losing your deposit. Your landlord might not want you tearing out that bathroom tile, even if it is terribly outdated.

However, there are inexpensive cosmetic changes you can make to any rental that don't require as much effort as you'd think and are easily reversible when you move out, if your landlord requires it. Here are some more ways to upgrade your rental without spending too much of your time or money.

## INSTALL NEW CABINET HANDLES

Time: 30 minutes / Cost: Under $50
You probably already know how easy it is to swap out the old, outdated hardware on your cabinets, but interior designer Erica Leigh Reiner suggests making a bold statement with your replacements.

"Replace and match the hardware on your cabinets, doors and furniture with unusual alternatives," she said. " Try leather pulls, stone, glass pulls, or classy acrylic and metal combos for a unique alternative to the stainless steel everyone gets."

Most cabinet handles and knobs will cost you less than $5. It's a small, inexpensive change that can have a big impact. Best of all, it's easy enough to reinstall the old hardware when you're ready to move out. "Just put the landlord's hardware somewhere for safekeeping," Ms. Reiner said.

## UPGRADE THE LIGHTING
Time: 1 hour / Cost: $50–$200

Most apartments come with ceiling mount light fixtures that can be easily replaced without rewiring anything at all: Simply pick out your new fixture, unscrew the old one, and replace it with your new, better fixture. If rewiring is involved—perhaps you want to switch a ceiling mount into a pendant light fixture, for example—make sure to shut off the electricity at your fuse box or circuit breaker first.

For an even easier project, simply swap out the light bulbs. Changing the brightness and temperature of your bulbs can completely change the look of a room, and you can find information about both brightness and temperature directly on the bulb box.

While you're thinking about changing the bulbs, consider upgrading to smart lighting. You get the benefit of light bulbs you can change to different colors, controlled with an app on your phone or tablet or even by voice control like Alexa on the Amazon Echo or by saying "Hey, Google" to your Google Home.

Grant Clauser, an editor at The Wirecutter, explained they're ideal for savvy renters. "Smart lighting, especially smart bulb, outlet plugs and strip lights, are easy additions for renters because you don't need to install anything permanently or do any

wiring," Mr. Clauser said. "Smart bulbs can be automated to turn on and off based on the time of day, motion sensors or triggers from other smart devices."

He also explained that even if you use lamps, smart lights can be set up in groups that give you the ability to turn off all the lights in a room—or your whole home—before bed. Best of all, you can get all of those features and then take them with you when it's time to move.

## REPLACE LIGHT SWITCH PLATES
Time: 1 hour / Cost: Under $50

If your rental comes with old, outdated electrical and light switch plates, it's easy enough to replace those, and most plates will cost you less than $5 apiece.

If you're willing to spend a bit more, you could upgrade your electrical outlets and light switches, too. Dimmer switches and USB outlets are relatively easy to install, and the package should include step-by-step instructions. In general, you'll have to remove the wiring connected to the old outlet and rewire it to the new outlet terminals. One word of caution: Make sure to shut off the electricity to the outlet via your circuit breaker or fuse panel and use a voltage tester to make sure there's no power going to the outlet while you're working on it. For easier installation and smart-home integration, you could opt for wireless switches.

Keep the old outlets on hand and replace them when you move out. Along with the other fixtures you replace, you can take them with you to the next place you rent.

## SWAP OUT THE FAUCET

Time: 2 hours / Cost: $100–$200

Most kitchen and bathroom sink faucets are also relatively easy to replace. When replacing a faucet, first identify the mounting type.

Once you find another faucet you like that fits that mounting type, the box should include instructions to replace your old one. You'll need to shut off the water flowing to the sink, remove the water lines and connect them to the new sink.

While you're upgrading your bathroom, shower heads are even easier to install. Using a pair of pliers, remove the old shower head and the Teflon tape around it, apply new tape, then use the pliers to thread on your new shower head fixture.

### THREE TYPES OF FAUCET MOUNTINGS

**Single-hole**
A single unit that might have a single handle or two handles.

**Centerset**
Centerset mounts have three holes but come with a single mount.

**Widespread**
A widespread mount has three separate pieces: the spout and two handles.

## ADD TRIM

Time: 4 hours / Cost: $100–$200

Check with your landlord on this one, but if your rental doesn't come with crown molding or you just want to replace what you have, you can install this yourself and completely change the look of a room.

"Adding border trim as a baseboard, crown molding, or a chair rail (wall trim) can subtly add a refined look to any room without breaking the bank," Ms. Reiner said. "Even adding trim and building out the frame and depth of your window frames or the face of your doors will instantly upgrade the look and feel of a space."

This fix requires a bit more handiwork, but it's still a doable project if you have a few hours and the right tools (you'll need a nail gun and compressor as well as a miter saw).

"It doesn't even have to be a gaudy, Victorian style molding; a simple and single shape, single depth piece of molding will do the trick," Ms. Reiner added.

## USE TILE STICKERS

Time: 1 hour / Cost: $100–$200

"Tile stickers are the easiest and the cheapest way to transform a kitchen or bathroom," said Eva Bowker, a writer who covers home improvement at Fantastic Handyman. "They come in different shapes, sizes and colors. They go right above the existing tiles and are easily detachable."

Of course, tile stickers won't have quite the same polished look of real tile, but they come in a variety of designs and there are plenty of unique, high-end options to choose from.

"The renovation project is quick, mess-free and only takes a couple of minutes," Ms. Bowker said.

"The stickers are easy to clean and can be efficiently removed by using some heat with a hair dryer and they peel off."

## CREATE A "FEATURE WALL"

**Time: 1–3 hours / Cost: Varies, depending on the project**

You can add some uniqueness to a cookie-cutter apartment with a feature wall: a wall that's decorated in such a way that it stands out and immediately catches your attention. You can achieve this with a simple coat of paint in a bold color or a gallery of photos, for example.

However, for an even more customized look, "create a feature element that looks built in," Ms. Reiner suggested. "This could be a wall-to-wall, up high bookshelf, a wall-to-wall curtain backdrop, or a wall-to-wall up high plant shelf. This creates a wow factor and looks like your home came with this feature."

## REPLACE THE TOILET

**Time: 1 hour / Cost: $100–$200**

For less than $50 and 60 minutes, you can replace your rental's well-worn toilet seat. That said, it's easier and more affordable than you might think to swap out the entire toilet, and it will instantly make your bathroom feel just a little less lived-in (always a good thing).

Check with your landlord to make sure it's OK, but chances are, they'll be happy to have you upgrade their rental. You might even try haggling this upgrade into your lease—save yourself some work and ask your landlord if the toilet can be replaced before you move in.

If you opt to do this yourself, you'll need a utility knife (and a fair amount of upper body strength) to remove the old toilet and caulk to seal the new one. Find a tutorial online to guide you through the project.

You may not be able to go full-on "Fixer Upper" with your rental, but these small projects will transform your space in an impactful way. And best of all, there's no demolition required.

> *Check with your landlord to make sure it's OK, but chances are, they'll be happy to have you upgrade their rental.*

# How to Clean Your Home the Smart Way

## BY JOLIE KERR

**THERE IS NO CORRECT WAY TO CLEAN A HOME,** and no hard and fast rules of housekeeping that can be applied across all dwellings. There are, however, some basics that are universal enough to provide a framework that can be modified to fit the unique needs of your home and lifestyle. It's also true that time is the enemy of cleaning, and that the simplest way to make cleaning easier is to not put it off. Here's a basic routine that will get you started.

## IN THE KITCHEN
### Keep Dishes and Sink Clean
If you're a person who tends to let dishes pile up in the sink to avoid washing them, try this simple trick to put the effort involved into perspective: For a few days, as you think of it, set a timer before you begin washing the dishes, and make note of how long it took to clean up. If you know the task will take just minutes to complete, it will be less difficult to convince yourself to take care of those dishes now.

**How to Clean a Burned Pot:** To clean a badly scorched pot without scrubbing, cover the burned area with a liberal amount of baking soda and pour in enough boiling water to fill the pot a third to halfway up. When the water is cool enough to touch, head in with your sponge and use the baking soda solution to scrub away the scorch. Dump the solution and wash the pot with hot, soapy water.

**The Dishwasher Debate:** While there isn't an absolutely correct way to load a dishwasher (and what would couples bicker over if such a directive were carved in stone?), there is one universal rule: It is much easier to load from back to front.

**Clean Your Sink:** The sink, especially the faucet, can be wiped free of bacteria and food particles with an all-purpose cleaner. And we all should probably clean the faucet more often, considering it's something we touch with raw-chicken-covered hands.

Sponges should be cleaned frequently, too, by running them through either the dishwasher or microwave. If you use a microwave, first make sure the sponge does not contain any metal, then get the sponge very wet and nuke it for two minutes; be careful when you remove it, as it will be quite hot.

Has your sponge holder developed mold or bacterial buildup? Use a toothbrush dipped in bleach or white vinegar—but never both, as the combination creates a dangerous chemical reaction—to scrub away mold. Follow by washing the sponge caddy with hot, soapy water or running it through the dishwasher.

## Keep Surfaces Clean

Wipe your counter and stovetops with an all-purpose cleaner after use. Stovetops in particular benefit from this type of regular, quick cleaning, as splatters, drips and grease become baked on when left too long.

**How to Clean a Stovetop:** Something tough will be required to scour away baked-on splatters and greasy film. A nonscratch scrubbing sponge combined with a gentle powder cleanser will make short work of stubborn messes. When cleaning stainless steel, scrub with the grain, rather than in a circular motion, to avoid scratching, and use a gentle touch, allowing the product, rather than force, to do the bulk of the cleaning work.

**How to Clean Small Appliances:** The exterior of small appliances like toasters, coffeemakers and blenders that sit out on countertops should be wiped frequently using all-purpose cleaners to prevent the buildup of splatters and greasy film from cooking. For deeper cleaning, take off all removable parts and wash the appliance by hand or in the dishwasher. Give the exterior a once-over with all-purpose cleaner using tools like cotton swabs or an old toothbrush to get into tight corners and other hard-to-reach spots.

## Tackle the Refrigerator

An easy way to keep tabs on a refrigerator is to add one simple task to your trash day routine:

When bagging up the garbage, open the fridge and eye its contents. Are there leftovers that have gone bad? Toss them. Has any produce liquefied in the crisper drawer? Dump it. Are the last few eggs in the carton about to go off? Make a note to have omelets for dinner, and congratulate yourself for being mindful of not wasting food.

**How to Clean Spills in the Refrigerator:** When sticky spills happen in the fridge or pantry, make short work of cleaning them by making a compress. Soak a sponge or rag in very hot water (mind your hands) and wring it so that it's not dripping. Then, press it onto the sticky spot until the compress begins to lose its heat. If the sticky spill has loosened sufficiently, wipe it away; if it's still clinging stubbornly, repeat as needed until the substance loosens up, and then wipe clean.

## Take Out the Trash in a Timely Fashion
Here is a hard truth: Time will not make your trash situation better. Take care of it now.

## HOW TO CLEAN THE BATHROOM
If ever there was a place where regular cleaning—once a week, once every other week, depending on use—makes your life better, it's in the bathroom. Wait longer, and it turns into a disgusting job.

## Scrub the Shower and/or Tub, Sink and Toilet
Many products designed for cleaning the shower and/or tub, sink and toilet do much of the work for you, provided you let them. The instructions will tell you how best to apply a product and for how long to let it work before wiping or scrubbing away. It's always a good idea to test a new product on an inconspicuous spot to ensure that it doesn't cause discoloration.

**How to Clean Tile and Grout:** Let the product do the work for you. Apply a mold- and mildew-eliminating product and let it penetrate the grout before hitting the surface with a stiff-bristled scrub brush. This will make much shorter work of what can be a tedious and exhausting chore.

**How to Remove Soap Scum:** Water spots and soap scum that build up on glass shower doors can drive you crazy, but try this strange tip: Wet a dryer sheet and scrub the glass in a circular motion. A milky white film will form, which can be wiped away using water and a squeegee, paper towels or a microfiber cloth. The dryer sheet doesn't need to be new; you can press a dryer sheet that's been used for laundry into double duty for this task.

## Hair Management
Hair is a particular issue in bathrooms. In general, hair pickup should be a dry proposition. Start by vacuuming, sweeping or dry mopping; if you introduce, say, a wet mop to a hairy floor, you'll end up with wet strands stuck to the floor. In the sink and around the toilet bowl, use paper towels or rags to pick up hairs before you introduce liquid cleansers.

**How to Keep Bathroom Floors Clean:** Store a small handheld vacuum in the bathroom to make staying on top of loose hairs a cinch.

## HOW TO CLEAN YOUR BEDROOM

A little effort makes a big difference in the bedroom. Simply making the bed and moving mugs and glasses to the kitchen every morning will do wonders for creating the appearance of a tidy bedroom.

### Make Your Bed

At the risk of unleashing your latent sullen teenager, it must be said that making the bed every day is a good habit. Would you like some reasons?

- It makes the bedroom look pulled together, and that's nice to come home to.
- If you have pets, making the bed helps to keep hair, dander and drool off your sheets.
- Turning down the bed at night is a ritual that can signal to the brain that it's time for sleep.
- Getting into a made bed just feels so good!

**It's Also Worth Saying This:** Many people think that making the bed is a waste of time, and that's OK. We're not all moved by the same things, and what a tidy-looking bed does for one person it may not do for another.

If you prefer to let the bed linens air out during the day, make the bed with the sheets exposed by folding the blanket and top sheet halfway down toward the foot of the bed.

### Put Clothes Away

Make putting away your freshly laundered clothes part of laundry day. You wouldn't bring bags of groceries into the house, set them down in front of the refrigerator and call it a day. Same with clean clothes: Part of laundry duty is putting them away.

### Keep Surfaces Clean

A feather duster may seem like a relic of the past, but in a bedroom—where we often use dresser tops and bedside tables to store books, eyeglasses, remote controls, etc.—that duster will make quick work of eliminating dust from knickknack-laden surfaces. The nature of gravity being what it is, dust first, vacuum second.

If you enjoy a cup of tea in the evening or leave a glass of water by the bed in case you get thirsty in the night, make a habit of moving it to the kitchen in the morning to prevent dirty dishes from littering your bedroom by the end of the week.

Invest in a bedside table that has a drawer. It will allow you to stash small items like hand cream and lip balm so that they're not cluttering up surfaces.

## HOW TO CLEAN YOUR FLOORS

When it comes to keeping the floors clean, it's as important to know what not to use as it is to know what to use.

### Your Basic Tools

The basic tools in a floor cleaning arsenal: vacuum, mop (wet, dry or steam) and broom. And, while absolutely no one wants to hear this, there is a lot to be said for getting down on your hands and knees to do the floors with a scrub brush and rags.

### How to Clean Carpet

If you have carpet or area rugs in your home, owning a vacuum is pretty much non-negotiable. The best vacuum is the one you'll use frequently, which sounds facile, but the most souped-up vacuum in

# HOW TO MAKE A HOSPITAL CORNER

Do you love a tightly tucked bed? Hospital corners are easy to master, once you know the steps to take:

**1**

Spread the flat sheet over the bed, with overhang on the sides and foot of the bed.

**2**

Starting at the foot of the bed, tuck the sheet tightly under the mattress.

**3**

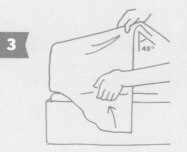

Take the sheet on one side of the bed and lift it up, creating a 45-degree fold up the side of the mattress. Then, tuck the excess fabric under the mattress.

**4**

Bring the lifted portion down, square the lines with the corner of the mattress and tuck it tightly.

**Repeat these four steps on the other side of the bed.**

# HOW TO CLEAN THE LIVING ROOM

**The name of the game in the living room is tidying and straightening.**

## REMOVE THAT WHICH DOES NOT BELONG

The nature of the living room being what it is, items that do not necessarily belong in the living room often make their way in there. Items such as dirty socks, wineglasses and even Krazy Glue eventually should be put in their rightful places (the hamper, dishwasher and toolbox, respectively).

## STRAIGHTEN AND SQUARE

Don't underestimate the impact that taking a minute or two to fluff cushions, fold throw blankets and straighten decorative pillows can have on the look of your living room. Similarly, squaring up stacks of magazines and books is a fast and easy way to create the appearance of a tidy space. A quick pass of the feather duster over bookshelves and coffee tables will help get rid of dust with little fuss; microfiber cloths will eliminate fingerprints and smudges in a flash.

the world is no good to you if it's too heavy to lift out of its storage space. For stains, a carpet and upholstery cleaner is a good thing to have when inevitable spills happen.

## How to Clean Wood Floors

Before you can clean wood flooring, try this trick to figure out if you have surface-sealed, or oil- or penetrating-sealed wood floors: Run your finger across the floor. If there's a smudge, the floors are oil- or penetrating-sealed; if not, they're surface-sealed.

When cleaning surface-sealed wood floors, avoid very hot water and abrasive cleaners. Use warm water to dilute dish soap, white vinegar or ammonia for these floors. Glass cleaner also works well. Oil- or penetrating-sealed wood should be cleaned with a broom or dry mop and vacuumed; avoid products that contain acrylic or water-based wax.

## How to Clean Laminate Floors

Laminate flooring should not be cleaned with soap, abrasives or products that contain abrasives. Instead, clean the floors routinely with a dry or damp mop. If a cleaning solution is needed, diluted ammonia or white vinegar can be used sparingly.

## How to Clean Linoleum Floors

Linoleum should also not be cleaned using very hot water, abrasives or wax- or solvent-based products. Instead, clean the floors routinely with a dry or damp mop. If a cleaning solution is needed, diluted ammonia or white vinegar can be used sparingly.

## How to Clean Tile and Natural Stone Floors

Tile and natural stone flooring should never be cleaned using abrasives or a vacuum with a brush roll attachment, both of which can cause scratching, nicking or cracking. The brush roll is a rotating brush that's great on carpeting for getting deep into fibers, but it shouldn't be used on hard surfaces. Ceramic and porcelain tile can be cleaned using oxygen bleach, chlorine bleach or diluted dish soap.

## HOW TO CLEAN YOUR CAR

The car is often treated like a living room on wheels. Clean and tidy as often as you prefer, but when it comes to cleaning up spills, don't delay.

## How to Clean Your Car's Floors and Seats

A handheld vacuum will do wonders for the interior of your car, without requiring a whole lot of work on your part, making it possibly the most crucial tool to own if you want to keep a tidy-looking vehicle. Pet hair, Cheerios, dirt and gravel, stray French fries and so on will be gone in no time, and you'll be surprised at what a simple vacuuming can do for the appearance of the seats, especially ones covered in fabric upholstery.

**How to Clean Stains on Car Upholstery:** Stains on fabric seats can be removed using an upholstery cleaner. It can be helpful to use the cleaning agent in concert with a white or light-colored rag, which will allow you to see how much of the stain you're picking up. Upholstery cleaner can also be used to clean stains from the headliner (the fabric-covered interior roof), but it's important to apply the cleaner to a rag, rather than directly to the headliner, which shouldn't be saturated with liquid. Use the rag to gently scrub in the direction of the grain, and let the headliner air dry before repeating if needed. Leather seats and interior detail can be cleaned using leather conditioner or, in the case of very bad stains, saddle soap. When choosing a product to clean leather seats, look to leather shoe cleaners (you may even have one already).

**How to Clean Your Dashboard:** Be careful when choosing dashboard cleaning products, as many can cause glare. Avoid any products that contain ammonia or alcohol, which can cause cracking. Simple as it sounds, the best thing to use to clean a dashboard is a damp microfiber cloth. For stubborn stains, add a small amount of dish soap to the cloth. Vents can also be wiped clean using a damp cloth, and a dry paintbrush or toothbrush can be used to remove dust and crumbs from vents and control buttons.

## How to Remove Odors from Your Car

When your car takes on a terrible odor, forget dangling trees from the rearview mirror and opt for a canister- or brick-style odor eliminator, like the Bad Air Sponge or Innofresh Auto Odor Eliminator. Good old Lysol is also excellent at quickly deodorizing and disinfecting the interior of the car or trunk.

## NOOKS AND CRANNIES

Compressed air can be used to blow crumbs, hair or dust from hard-to-clean spaces like cupholders and door side pockets. Sticky spills that have dried can be given the same hot compress treatment as sticky spills in the fridge: Wet a sponge or rag with very hot water, being careful not to burn your hand, and press it on the spill until it begins to loosen, at which point it can be wiped away. Keep a pack of bathroom wipes in your car for quickly addressing spills, on both hard and upholstered surfaces.

## What is your home's dirty little secret?

When my clients are ordering something for their homes or offices, I tell them that they should have whatever it is installed as soon as they get it, otherwise they just won't do it. I definitely don't follow that advice. I ordered ceiling fans this summer that are still in the box. It's December now, and they've been sitting in my hallway for months. And in my office, I have a box of shelves that's probably been there for a year. It's always the finishing touches of a project—you get 99 percent done, and the last part is hardest to complete. I don't know when I'll put up the fans. Now I might as well wait until it's summer again! It's absurd.

— **Dani Arps,** founder of Dani Arps Interior Design

The hardest thing for me to keep organized in my own home is without a doubt paper. That's because papers are not just a physical organizing issue; each piece of paper represents a time demand of some sort (read, reconcile, pay, investigate, order, decide)—and I have such a low patience for this kind of administrative tedium in life. So, I do kind of procrastinate on it, and it can pile up. When things come in the mail, I'm like...what do I do with this? I collect it in the office area of the home in a box that's on the credenza. First it sits on top, then I move it inside the credenza, and I'm like, I really need to go through this, and I don't.

— **Julie Morgenstern,** organizing and productivity expert and author of six books, including *Organizing from the Inside Out* and her latest, *Time to Parent*

I'm completely incapable of decorating. I advocate for making your bed every day, and I run about 90 percent of that. I try to keep my kitchen counter as clean as possible, but I looked at it last night, and it was a mountain of disaster. When I'm writing a book, nothing gets done. But every day, you have a chance to start over again. It's not a pass-fail course. I encourage people to be a little bit more forgiving of themselves.

— **Rachel Hoffman,** author of *Unf*ck Your Habitat: You're Better Than Your Mess* and *Cleaning Sucks: An Unf*ck Your Habitat Journal for Less Mess, Less Stress, and a Home You Don't Hate,* out in January 2020.

# Stain Removal 101

## BY JOLIE KERR

**STAINS ARE AN UNAVOIDABLE SIDE EFFECT OF LIFE**—but with the right tools, they don't have to stick around.

There are many, many good options when it comes to stain removal, and if we tried to catalogue every one of them, we'd be here all day. These are some of the best solutions and techniques to use with the most common stains that befoul our belongings.

## DINGY AND SWEAT-STAINED WHITES

It's tempting to reach for the bleach when a white tee or set of white sheets has gone yellow from age, sweat or the havoc that aluminum-containing antiperspirants wreak on the armpits of our shirts. But skip the bleach—or at least skip the chlorine stuff—and opt instead for oxygen bleach. Use it in addition to detergent to keep dinginess and staining at bay. When the inevitable dinginess brought on by age and wear occurs, dilute a large scoop in hot water and soak yellowed whites or lights for an hour up to overnight, then launder as usual.

## REMOVING BLOOD

There are a million (rough count) methods for removing bloodstains, so here I'll keep it to just a few: Hydrogen peroxide is one of the most common options, and it's very good, but it's critical that you test it in an inconspicuous place to ensure it won't cause color loss. Unseasoned meat tenderizer (really!) diluted with water to form a paste is excellent on older, set-in bloodstains. Salt water or saline solution is great on the fly because salt and water are pretty easy to find, even when you're far from your laundry supplies. And in a pinch, saliva can work, if you can handle the gross-out factor.

## CHOCOLATE

Weird but true: Shout spray is incredible at removing chocolate stains. Spray a small amount on the stain, massage it using your fingers, and marvel as the stain dissolves.

## RED WINE, CRANBERRY, BLUEBERRY

I refer to this deadly trio of stains as "the reds," which may not be exactly precise, since the stains are more purple than red, but "the purples" sounds too regal for stains that are so common. A product called Wine Away will make short work of removing not only red wine stains but also those caused by cranberries and blueberries, whether whole or in juice or sauce form.

## OIL AND GREASE

If you catch a grease stain right as it happens, massage a small amount of diluted dish or hand soap into the spot using your fingers. For more stubborn stains, or ones you can't get to straight away, dab a bit of Lestoil or Pine-Sol onto the stains prior to laundering.

For especially bad grease stains, or for those that happen on materials that can't be laundered or don't love water (like silk or suede), reach for the cornstarch. Yes, cornstarch! The stuff you use to thicken pie filling is also amazing at absorbing grease.

To use it for stain removal:

- Lay the garment flat on a surface where it can stay, undisturbed, for 12 to 48 hours.
- Pile an anthill-style mound of cornstarch on the stain.
- Walk away.
- Come back after a bit and brush the cornstarch away and check out the stain. It's probably not there anymore! But if it is, and it's lightened significantly, simply repeat the process to allow the cornstarch more absorbing time.

## INK

Ink is a funny animal in the stain kingdom. It's one that does not necessarily benefit from immediate treatment. The problem with a fresh ink stain is that if you introduce any sort of liquid to it, there's a risk of flooding the stain and making it spread. So be

towels, but sometimes you need something extra to eliminate smells like mildew or body odor. White vinegar works and is especially effective on towels, where it will also serve as a natural fabric softener. **To use it:** Add a half to a full cup to the rinse cycle of the washing machine.

> White vinegar works and is especially effective on towels, where it will also serve as a natural fabric softener.

aware of that, but also be aware of this: Isopropyl alcohol (that's the rubbing stuff) is aces on ink stains and is what you should reach for when a pen accidentally swipes your shirt or the kids hit the couch with their markers.

## ODOR RETENTION

Using the right washer and dryer settings can help reduce odor retention in clothes and items like

While white vinegar also works quite well on athletic gear that's retained a musty odor, over time the acid can break down the elasticity. Opting for a sports detergent, such as Tide Plus Febreze Sport Odor Defense, or a booster that's used in concert with your regular detergent, like Tide Odor Rescue, will help to keep your favorite yoga pants or sweat-wicking shirt odor-free without breaking down the material.

# How to Preserve Your Family Memories, Letters and Trinkets

BY KELSEY McKINNEY

**DENISE LEVENICK IS HER FAMILY'S HISTORIAN.** She's not a professional archivist, but she's a well-practiced one, running a blog called The Family Curator, and always trying to learn more. But even her family makes mistakes.

A few years ago, Ms. Levenick's son lost almost everything of sentimental value to him when his washing machine blew out, a pipe burst and the plastic bin where he had put all of his old stamps and heirlooms for safekeeping became a pool of water where mold grew.

The accident, of course, couldn't have been prevented. But the damage to his beloved records could have been mitigated had he been slightly more strategic with his storage strategy. A breathable archival box, instead of a plastic bin, could have prevented water from puddling, and keeping that box in the closet, where there are no exposed pipes and little humidity, could have saved those precious heirlooms. But people often don't think about their family papers and keepsakes until it is too late.

Good archival practices might not be the most exciting of hobbies, but it could be the key to keeping your family history intact for future generations.

## STORING LOVE LETTERS, PHOTOGRAPHS AND OTHER IMPORTANT PAPERS

Recently, someone wrote to Mary Oey, a conservator at the Library of Congress, asking for help archiving her father's personal papers. He was a Holocaust survivor, and he had used his diaries and papers as primary sources to teach schoolchildren about his experience. He had laminated them to keep them safe, and—Ms. Oey gave a mournful sigh as she told this story—lamination is a terrible way to preserve documents. There was no way to save this patron's history.

"The only way to extricate paper from lamination is to use lots of solvents to dissolve the plastic," Ms. Oey said. "Some stiffer laminations, we don't know how to get off, and it doesn't protect the document. The lamination itself can ruin a document beyond repair."

Not only is the lamination process itself likely to harm delicate papers, it also places undue stress on objects that can cause them to tear, yellow or become brittle prematurely.

For items like papers and fragile documents, the best thing you can do is to control the environment they're stored in, said Maureen Callahan, an archivist for the Sophia Smith Collection at Smith College.

"Water and vermin are the greatest enemies of paper," Ms. Callahan said. "Folks also often store family records in basements or attics, where heat and humidity can fluctuate wildly and where water is more likely to enter."

Your best bet? Ms. Oey said it's a clean, dark space, like the top of a linen closet.

With items like printed photographs and albums, making things clean and neat will go a long way.

"Neatness for photographs is almost as important as storage," Ms. Oey said. Very important photographs can be stored in high-quality paper folders (check to make sure they are acid-free and lignin-free) or in good plastic sleeves like ones made of Mylar. But an important caveat to remember: Not using a sleeve is preferable to a cheap one that will scratch.

Every conservator who spoke to the *Times* recommended cardboard boxes over plastic bins for storage, because they don't breed mold as easily and they dry out more quickly. But if you want to get fancy, the best option is to buy acid-free archival boxes, online or from vendors like the Container Store. They can be a bit pricey, but hold up best against moisture and mold.

And just as important as knowing what to do is knowing what not to do.

"All conservators would agree with me when I say we have seen miles and miles of terrible sticky tape," Ms. Oey said.

So remember:

- No tape (it sticks).
- No paper clips or staples (they can rust).
- Definitely no lamination.
- And absolutely no plastic bins that can fill up with water.

## BEYOND PAPER (WEDDING DRESSES, RECORD COLLECTIONS AND MORE)

Family archives can include all sorts of strange ephemera. Maybe your grandmother had an extensive record collection, or there's a box of photo slides sitting in your garage that you have no idea what to do with.

Whatever the case, individual items like these don't have any catchall rules besides common sense. But Ms. Oey encourages individuals with archiving goals they don't know how to accomplish to seek out experts who are available.

Most libraries have an online reference system called Ask a Librarian that allows individuals to talk

## DIGITIZING THOSE LOVE LETTERS AND PRINTED PHOTOS

Just as with paper archives, the most important part of archiving digital files is storage.

"How you store your files and where will always be the most important form of preservation anyone can do," Ms. Oey said. Computers, for example, are not safe in and of themselves. Anything important to you should never have only one digital file.

> " 
> *Audio and video preservation are often neglected by family archivists because they are more technical than common sense, but they are no less important.*

to preservationists who can advise them on how to best take care of the strange item, or point them toward an expert who can provide assistance, or help them find a conservator who might mend the item (though that can get pricey). A great place to start is the Library of Congress website.

And that old wedding dress that's still in the closet? It's best to let a professional preservationist handle it, experts said. The Association of Wedding Gown Specialists has a list of guidelines and recommendations on its site. (Though if you still want to go it alone, the same rules apply: Have a professional clean it, then store it in an acid-free box in a cool, dark space away from water.)

The key with digital archiving, archivists say, is duplication. Every important file should have three copies. Ideally, those three copies should be stored on at least two different storage media. Ms. Levenick said that she personally uses a 3-2-1 method for backing up: three copies, two different media and at least one away from home. For example, you might store two digital wedding albums on your desktop and in a cloud-based storage.

The first step to a good digital practice is high-resolution photographs. Ms. Oey recommends snapping photos of your items in good (preferably natural) light. "If you have a nice digital camera like an SLR, that's great, but honestly an iPhone [or other smartphone] will work just fine." Any smartphone camera will do.

The second step is storing those files just as safely as the original documents. While your digital photographs aren't going to get soaked through by a burst pipe, keeping them in well-maintained environments is equally important.

"If you are using physical storing, you need to regularly migrate off one hard disk and onto another," Ms. Oey said. That includes hard drives, flash drives, CDs and anything else. "Doing this every three to five years on average will keep your files safe and up to date."

## DIGITIZING AUDIO, VIDEO AND EVERYTHING ELSE

Audio and video preservation are often neglected by family archivists because they are more technical than common sense, but they are no less important.

Audio recordings—like reel-to-reel, cassette, mini-tapes from answering machines—can be easily translated to digital form as MP3 files, but not in a high enough quality to replace the original recording. Several archivists said that you could spend anywhere from $400 to $40,000 digitizing audio, and that letting a vendor handle it is definitely the way to go (unless you want to make a hobby of digitization).

But if you have a large collection, it'll be more expensive. Many vendors charge around $15 to digitize a cassette. The Association for Recorded Sound Collections has a list of vendors and plenty of resources on preserving physical sound and digitizing it.

Preserving video follows many of the same rules. The trend is toward storing video in digital formats instead of carrier-dependent formats. Again, if you want to make a hobby of it, there's plenty of info to

## DO YOUR BEST, BUT DON'T ARCHIVE EVERYTHING

Preventive care of heirlooms is always easier than trying to repair a broken item.

"Death and decay is inevitable, and not everything is worth saving," Ms. Callahan said. Curation, everyone agreed, is maybe the most important part of archiving.

"Be discriminating," she said, adding that if record-keeping becomes overwhelming, "you're far less likely to go through them, and folks from the next generation probably won't know what to make of them."

dive into. But for those who just want their videos safe, vendor help is the way to go. Most video conversion vendors will charge you around 20 cents per foot for 8mm, Super 8mm and 16mm film conversion.

Turning to other heirlooms, vinyl records, for example, can be particularly dangerous and easy to destroy, so it's recommended that you take those to a local vendor. As with every other kind of archiving, if you have something weird or uncommon, it's probably best to call an archivist and grab some specialized tips.

# The Annual Home Maintenance Checklist

BY RONDA KAYSEN

**GIVEN THE OPTION,** few of us would volunteer to spend a Sunday on a ladder pulling leaves out of a gutter. But when your home is your biggest investment, as it is for most Americans, maintaining it is a must. Home maintenance can feel like a daunting chore—particularly for a new homeowner who's never seen a boiler up close, let alone drained one. But it doesn't have to feel overwhelming. A home operates with the seasons, coming to life in the spring and hunkering down in the winter. Follow this natural arc all year long, and keep on top of the small stuff, and your house will run like a well-oiled machine.

## SPRING

Come springtime, most of us are eager to throw open the windows and clean out the closets. It's also time to give your house, inside and out, a good once-over.

### The Outside of Your Home

**Goodbye, Snow Blower; Hello, Lawnmower:** With the last of the winter snowstorms behind you, early spring is the time to store your snow blower (if you have one) for the summer. You'll need to drain the fuel or add a stabilizer, and clean the motor. Later, pull out the lawnmower

> " Spring is a good time to give the house a good scrub, washing all the winter away.

and give it a checkup before the grass gets too long. Mowers get a lot of use, but not a lot of love. Send it out for a tune-up annually, where a small-engine repair company could sharpen the blades, change the spark plug and do any other necessary maintenance. Expect to spend $50 to $75, according to Angie's List.

**Inspect:** Walk around the outside of the house: Are there cracks in the concrete? Is the driveway in good condition? Check the roof for signs of loose or broken shingles. Look up at the chimney for signs of wear. Check the facade and foundation for cracks or signs of water pooling.

**The Gutters:** Your gutters control the flow of rainwater on your house, protecting your roof, siding and foundation. Clogged gutters can cause a roof to leak or water to infiltrate your house. Clean them at least twice a year (or more frequently, depending on how many trees surround your property and hang over your roof). Also, check for damage.

If you clean them yourself, be careful on that ladder, as more than 630,000 Americans needed medical treatment in 2015 for ladder-related injuries, according to the United States Consumer Product Safety Commission. You can also hire a professional gutter cleaner, a service that can cost $75 to $200, depending on the size of your home, according to Angie's List.

**Paint:** Exterior paint looks nice and protects your shingles from water damage and rot. Look for signs of peeling or chipping paint. You may need a touch-up or a fresh coat. If you plan to hire a professional, schedule the job in the spring so the work gets done by the end of the summer.

**Give the House a Bath:** Spring is a good time to give the house a good scrub, washing all the winter away. Take the storm windows off and wash the windows, inside and out. The house can get grimy, too. Grit stuck to the facade can damage paint and masonry over time. Wait for a warm, dry day and get to work. Here's how to clean your house's exterior:

- Close all windows and doors, and cover the ground and hedges with plastic sheeting.
- Avoid the instinct to rent a power washer, as it may not be necessary, and it could damage siding or masonry, depending on your building materials. In most cases, an ordinary garden hose will do.
- Attach a siding cleaning kit to the hose and get to work.
- Spot-clean heavily soiled areas. Use detergent sparingly, as it can harm your plants.

**Patio or Deck:** You may not use your deck all winter; chances are it has a layer of winter grime across it. Sweep it clean. Inspect your deck, looking for signs of cracked wood and loose nails. Pull out any leaves or debris from between the boards. Then clean it thoroughly:

- Wet the deck down with a garden hose.
- Spray it with water and a cleaning solution using a pump sprayer, and wait 10 minutes.
- Scrub it with a broom and spray it down with the garden hose again.
- Treat a wooden deck with borate for algae to protect against wood rot.
- Let the wood dry for a few days and then stain and seal it.

## Inside Your Home

**HVAC Systems:** For homes with central heat and air, call your HVAC technician to schedule the system's biannual checkup and servicing. A technician should check the ductwork for signs of damage, and clean and service the furnace and A/C compressor. Clean the bathroom vents, too. Cleaning ducts and vents costs homeowners an average $348, according to HomeAdvisor.

**Steam Heat:** For those of you with steam heat, drain your boiler to clear out any accumulated sediment.

**Plumbing:** Give your pipes a good once-over, checking under sinks to make sure there are no signs of leaks. Look up at your ceilings, too, for telltale water stains—a sign of a leak in the wall. Check faucets for drips and the flapper in the tank of your

### CHIMNEY CHECKUP

Even if you do not regularly use the fireplace, the chimney still needs a regular checkup. A chimney carries dangerous gases from your fireplace, wood stove or furnace out of your home, helping to keep the air inside breathable. Your chimney should be inspected annually, and cleaned periodically depending upon how often you use it, according to the National Fire Protection Association.

toilet to make sure it has not worn out. (Once the flapper starts to go, expect your toilet to run more frequently.) Fix what you can yourself; call a plumber for what you need help with.

**Sump Pump:** Spring often brings rain. Check your sump pump to make sure it's draining properly. You do not want to wait until a major snow thaw or rainstorm to find out that the pump's motor is shot.

**Check Your Smoke Alarm and Carbon Monoxide Detectors:** Between 2007 and 2011, almost two-thirds of home fire deaths were in homes without working smoke detectors, according to the National Fire Protection Association. Check and change batteries on your smoke and carbon monoxide detectors twice

a year. The switch to daylight saving time is a good day to choose for the job. Another good option: Mother's Day. You may also want to consider so-called smart detectors that are linked throughout your home and give voice alerts, not just alarms.

## SUMMER

Summer is the season to enjoy your home, not fix it. But still, some chores must be done. Keep on top of them, and you'll still have plenty of time for beer and barbecues.

### Outside Your Home

**Exterior Repairs:** If you plan to paint your facade or repair your porch, summer is a great time to get that done.

### Inside Your Home

**Ceiling Fans:** Reverse the setting on your ceiling fans to counterclockwise. This pushes the air down, creating a nice breeze.

**Air-Conditioning:** Whether you have central air-conditioning or window units, you should clean your filters at least once a month, particularly if you've been running the AC a lot.

**Plan for Extreme Heat:** Heat waves are inevitable in summer, so prepare your home before the harsh weather arrives. Check the weather stripping around doors and windows to keep the cool air in. Cover windows that receive morning or afternoon sun with drapes. Check on your neighbors, particularly older ones who live alone. Heat waves

## BUGS AND OTHER PESTS

You're not the only one who loves your home. Termites, ants, carpenter bees and mice like it, too. Some infestations, like a single trail of ants, may be resolved with a spray can and a thorough cleaning of the area. Others, like termites, demand professional assistance. A single visit from a pest control company could cost $300 to $550, according to HomeAdvisor. But if you have a continuing pest problem, like mice, consider an annual contract, with a monthly fee of around $40 to $45, according to HomeAdvisor. Discuss the details of the contract carefully, as not all services are included in a standard contract.

But you also need to be diligent and take steps to reduce the risk of infestation. Seal holes where mice and roaches can get in. Protect mattresses against invaders like bedbugs—if you go on a trip and think you may have brought unwanted stowaways home in your luggage, unpack in the garage and wash all your clothes immediately. Check the attic regularly to make sure a family of, say, raccoons has not taken up residence.

can strain power grids, causing brownouts and blackouts. Check your disaster supply kit to make sure it's fully stocked with items like batteries for flashlights, canned food, bottled water, medicines, a battery-powered radio and a first-aid kit.

## FALL

As the leaves begin to turn and the days cool, it's time to wind your house down for the winter. For those of you living in warmer climates, autumn does not necessarily deliver a giant to-do list.

### Outside Your Home

**Gutters:** Once the leaves fall, call your gutter company to get those gutters cleaned and inspected. Any repairs that need to be done on the gutters or downspouts should happen before winter sets in. Your workers should also inspect the roof for any loose or broken tiles. Schedule the job before you get a heavy snow, which could leave frozen leaves and debris in the gutters.

**Faucets and Hoses:** Before the first freeze, drain and shut off your outdoor faucets so that they do not freeze. Roll up your hoses and store them for winter.

**Sprinklers:** If you live in a cold climate, you need to shut your sprinkler system for the winter to protect it from harsh weather. Skip this step now, and come springtime you could have a hefty repair bill.

- Shut off the water supply to your irrigation system before freezing weather arrives.
- Insulate the main shutoff valve and any aboveground piping.

- Shut down the timer, if you have an automatic system.
- Drain the remaining water from the system.

**Firewood:** If you plan to use your fireplace this winter, stock up on seasoned firewood in the fall. Stack it on pallets, so it does not sit on the moist ground. Don't pack the wood too tightly or fungus could grow. Cover the wood with plastic sheeting, making sure it does not touch the ground, either. Wood can be stored in an unheated garage, but don't keep logs in your house for more than a week, as they could attract insects, according to Michigan State University Extension.

### Inside Your Home

**Air-Conditioning:** If you have central air, get the system serviced (you can do this at the same time that you service your furnace). Window units can stay in the window year round if they are sealed with no gaps. Cover the inside and the outside of the appliance to prevent drafts, provide insulation and protect the equipment from the elements. There are even some decorative options out there. But if you'd like your window back, or have concerns about drafts, remove the unit and store it for winter. Window units are heavy and unwieldy, so take it slowly. Store it upright, not on its side.

**Furnace and HVAC:** Get your furnace and ductwork serviced. A clean system will be more energy efficient, and an inspection will alert you to problems. Check and replace air filters, as necessary. Test your thermostat to make sure it works properly. Make sure heating vents are open and nothing is blocking them.

**Boilers and Radiators:** For homes heated with steam heat, the boiler is the tank that holds and heats the water. Call the plumber for its annual checkup. You should also drain water from the boiler to remove sediment that has collected and settled in the tank. Make sure the tank is refilled before you turn it on. A plumber or heating specialist can also check your radiators to make sure the valves are working properly and have not worn out. Check your thermostat, too.

**Chimney:** If you did not get your chimney cleaned and inspected in the spring, call a chimney sweep now and have it done before you start using your fireplace or your furnace.

**Windows and Doors:** Walk around the house and check windows and doors for drafts. Caulk door and window frames where necessary. In late fall, install storm windows and the glass panel on storm doors to keep the heat in and the cold out.

**Dryer Vent:** Clothes dryers cause 2,900 fires a year, with many fires happening in the fall and winter, according to the United States Fire Administration. Lint is a major culprit, so have your dryer vent inspected and cleaned annually by an HVAC specialist who specializes in ductwork or dryer vents.

**Smoke and Carbon Monoxide Detectors:** There's no harm in checking your detectors twice a year, so when you turn your clocks back to standard time, check your smoke and carbon monoxide detectors, too. Change the batteries.

## WINTER

For the most part, we hunker down in the winter, as the weather is often too cold and unpredictable to tackle major home improvement projects. Make sure your home is prepared for the harsh weather.

### Outside Your Home

**Bring Out the Snow Blower:** Make sure your snow blower is in good working order before it snows. You do not want to be caught in the first major storm with only an orange shovel to dig you out. Send the snow blower to a small-engine repair company for a tune-up. Some

### ICE DAMS

When ice accumulates along the eaves of your roof, it can cause a dam that can damage gutters, shingles and siding. As water leaks into your house, it can wreak havoc on your paint, your floors and your insulation. Throughout the winter, inspect the exterior of your home regularly for signs of ice dams. Look for icicles, because the same forces create dams. Consider buying a roof rake. The $30 tool will help keep ice off your roof in the first place by removing fresh snow from your roof after a storm. Do not hack away at the ice, as that could harm you or your roof.

companies will pick up and drop off your equipment for you. Expect to spend $60 to $200, depending on the size of your blower, according to Angie's List. Make sure you have gasoline and motor oil.

**Stock Up on Supplies:** Stock up on ice melt before the Weather Channel tells you a storm is coming. Pet owners and parents should shop carefully, as the chemicals in ice melt can harm pets and people alike, if ingested. Look for brands free of salt or chloride. But even products billed as "pet safe" can still harm your pet, so wipe their paws and don't let them lick treated snow. Ice-melting products can also damage your foliage, so use sparingly. Make sure your shovel survived last winter, because you will need to dig out stairways and narrow pathways, even if you have a blower.

## Inside Your Home

**Heating Systems:** Check and change filters on your heating system, as filters need to be replaced anywhere from twice a year to once a month. Keep an eye on the water levels in your boiler to make sure they do not fall too low.

**Frozen Pipes:** When water freezes in pipes, it expands, damaging or cracking the pipes. When the ice melts, and the pipe bursts, your home fills with water. Pipes near or outside the home are at greatest risk, like outdoor faucets, pipes in an unheated garage or swimming pool supply lines.

A few tips:

- Shut off and drain outdoor faucets before the cold weather hits.
- Insulate pipes where you can.
- On cold days and nights, keep the cabinets below sinks open to let warm air in.
- You can also run the faucet at a drip to keep water moving.
- Keep the thermostat set at a steady temperature.
- If you go away, set the thermostat to a minimum of 55 degrees, according to the American Red Cross.

**Generator:** A portable generator can provide you with a lifeline in a blackout. Power it up every three months, and have it serviced at least once a year (even if you never use it). Keep fuel and motor oil on hand in the event of a storm. Do not let fuel sit in the tank for long periods of time, as that can damage it. Check it regularly for corrosion and wear.

**Winter Storm Prep:** A heavy winter storm can leave you housebound for days. Stock up on wood for the fireplace, gas for the snow blower and canned food and bottled water, in case you lose power. Check your emergency supply kit for batteries, a radio, a first-aid kit and any medicines you may need. Check on neighbors who may need help shoveling out (a little camaraderie in a storm goes a long way).

# How to Host a Dinner Party

BY LAURA RYSMAN

**FOOD, DRINK, FRIENDS, GOOD CONVERSATION**—a dinner party is, in the end, a simple and enduring combination of ingredients, made unique by what hosts and guests infuse the evening with. To help you achieve a more flawless and fun-filled gathering, here are a set of guidelines with everything you need to know about throwing your best dinner party.

## FIRST, MAKE A TIMELINE

Advance planning will ultimately make a dinner party that much easier to pull off. Making accurate lists and giving yourself plenty of time for each task will minimize chaos and help you tackle the inevitable glitches that arise.

The British party planner Fiona Leahy says that as a professional, outsourcing is key for her own busy life; but even if you can't hire a catering staff for your private affair, think about what you don't have to do yourself—like picking up a dessert, having wine, flowers or other supplies delivered, or hiring a cleaning service for before or after the party. Keeping it simple for yourself is crucial. "I'm not above just serving a sourdough truffle pizza with great wine," Ms. Leahy says. "It's the company that counts...and, of course, the tablescape." Here, her timeline tips for your party:

## Two weeks before:

- Create your guest list, making sure you have enough dishes to serve everyone.
- Send out your invitations.
- Think about the atmosphere and aesthetic you'd like for the evening. Figure out what you'll need for décor and make a list.

## One week before:

- Pin down confirmations from guests, and be sure to check on their dietary restrictions.
- Plan your menu, keeping in mind what ingredients are in season and what can be prepared a day before the party.
- Think about how you'll want your dishes to look when served, and be sure to include any special tools, plates or garnishes you'll need to create.
- Pick up candles and any other décor (except flowers) you'll want for the evening.

## Two days before:

- Pick up all the ingredients for the dinner.
- Purchase wine and any other beverages you'll be serving, and make sure you have a good corkscrew.
- Fill up your ice trays and pick up extra ice from the store if you'll be making cocktails.
- Make a playlist (or several).

## The day before:

- Prepare as much of the food as possible, including dessert.
- Clean up your home, especially areas where guests will be (the dining room, living room and bathroom) and be sure the trash and the dishwasher are empty for the next day.
- Pick up flowers or other natural touches and put them in vases.

## The day of:

- Take it from pro chefs and prepare a *mise en place*, setting out all of the ingredients, sauces and garnishes you'll need to finish your dishes around a counter area with a cutting board and good knives. Line up small bowls and fill them with everything you'll need.
- Prepare any last dishes.
- Set up the table and any décor. All linens, table settings, glasses, place cards and candles should be laid out at this point.

## Two hours before:

- Arrange all the food you cooked previously on the counter and pull out any pots you'll need to prepare them.
- Set up a drink and snack station for guests' arrival with wine or an aperitif and something small to nibble on.
- Put pitchers or bottles of water on the table.
- Get dressed for the evening.
- Light candles and put on your first playlist.
- Have a glass of wine or take a moment for yourself so you're relaxed when your guests arrive.

## DINNER PARTY INVITATIONS

An invitation lets your guests know you're planning something special for them and helps mark the difference between a regular dinner and a dinner party. Yours should reflect the aesthetic of your evening and the level of formality you wish to communicate. If you're picturing a more formal dinner, send a printed or handwritten invitation.

## How to Send an E-Vite

There are a number of easy online options that allow you to quickly create invitations and send them to your guests, as well as keep track of your RSVP's. If you're connected to all of your invitees on Facebook, the site's event-creation option is quick and straight-forward. Other sites help you create e-vites that mimic the feel of old-fashioned paper invitations

> 66
>
> *Send the invitations as soon as possible—*
> *the more notice you give your guests,*
> *the more likely they'll be able to come.*

For more casual events, an email or e-vite can work. Send the invitations as soon as possible—the more notice you give your guests, the more likely they'll be able to come. Ask guests to RSVP and follow up to be sure they received the invitation.

When considering your invites, remember that today paper post is a rarity and makes a statement of real intent, so reserve it for when you are planning a significant or fancier evening. Even the New York invitation designer Ellen Weldon says she just phones up her guests for an intimate dinner party. But, she says, "for larger events, I send gloriously lettered invitations!"

She also sends thank-you notes to her guests for special occasions. It's a good idea for guests to send their own thank-you to their hosts the day after the dinner, whether that's a text, email, phone call or handwritten note.

with some technological benefits, such as Google maps of the location and automatic reminders for your guests to RSVP. We all know about Evite. It's a no-fail option. But Paperless Post offers free and premium designs with the option to order printed versions. Pingg features a range of original work by artists and Punchbowl offers organizing tools like date-planning with your friends, but both will hit your invitees with ads unless you pay a membership fee.

## How to Craft a Guest List

Consider your guest list before you send the invitations. How many people can fit comfortably in your space? Can you prepare enough food for the number of guests you're inviting? Is there anyone on your list who won't get along with others or is likely to cause problems at the dinner? Have you included a friend or two who will give you a hand during the party if needed—and who can help facilitate conversation? Will the people on your list mesh well together, even if they don't yet know each other?

## CHOOSE YOUR DINNER PARTY ATMOSPHERE

In order to create the atmosphere you'd like for your evening, first think about the details of dinners you've been to where you enjoyed yourself, and then think about the kind of night you hope this will be: Formal or relaxed? Calm or boisterous? Intimate or packed with new acquaintances? This is very much about who you are and what you want your guests to experience. Everything from the look of your table to the décor to the music playing during the evening will impact that experience, so be sure that you are able to describe the atmosphere you want in a few words, and then apply the theme to all of these areas. "Decorations should reflect your personality," says Angela Missoni, creative director of the Missoni brand. Indulge guests in your own taste rather than thinking about what's proper.

When Missoni planned the celebration for her 20th anniversary in charge of the brand, she was so committed to re-creating a warm, welcoming feel that she brought in truckloads of colorful vintage furniture and decorations from her own house to the party space. "It has to feel like home," she says. "I was raised in these intimate dinners of my parents and I learned to love creating these events." Her approach? "Very informal, and very friendly. Even if there's a professional side to the occasion, I have the dinners because they're fun, because they're the best way to meet people."

### CHANGE THE LIGHTING

Turn off a few lamps and light plenty of candles. Whether you use a silver candelabra or a handful of tea lights, soft illumination is one of the easiest and most important ways you can transform your space. "If you've just got yourself a six-pack of beer and some candles, you've got yourself a great party," counsels designer Sara Ruffin Costello.

### Set the Table

Think of your tablescape as more than just serving accouterments for food and drinks—it is, in fact, the scenery for the theater of dinner that you are crafting. Your table linens, plates, silverware, glasses and decorations are visual clues to your guests. Traditional styles create a refined ambience; a colorful mix will create a more lighthearted one.

Martina Mondadori Sartogo, the editor of the maximalist design magazine *Cabana*, advises that to create a tablescape you should start with a tablecloth you like—and build up the look you want from there. Her own style—"the opposite of matchy-matchy"—blends eclectic flea market plates and glasses with family heirlooms, Murano glass and even the occasional find from Zara Home, along with an assortment of vintage cutlery and custom-made printed tablecloths. "The table is a way of expressing your personality," she says. "Mine is not very formal." Mixing up flea market finds is not the only way to set a table but, as Mondadori Sartogo sees it, "The mood right now is to have fun decorating and not be too stiff."

For inspiration, search for images of table settings online, on Pinterest and on Instagram—there are endless ways to use dishes, napkins, place cards, candelabras, centerpieces, tablecloths and decorations to create a unique and striking tablescape.

## CREATING A DINNER PARTY MENU

While you may think that a dinner party requires extraordinary feats of cooking to impress your guests, the most important aspect of your menu is that it can be prepared almost entirely before any guests arrive, freeing you up to host.

Rita Sodi, chef and owner of the Tuscan-inspired New York restaurant I Sodi, recommends creating your menu around a special ingredient that's just come into season such as truffles, asparagus, artichokes, tomatoes or pumpkin, which lends a dinner a more celebratory dining spirit (and tastier food).

Sodi will sometimes throw cooking parties where she invites everyone into the kitchen, with a case of wine on the countertop, to help her prepare dishes. But unless you want your whole party in the kitchen, make sure you're serving dishes that allow you to spend as much time as possible at the hub of the evening—the table. "A tavola non si invecchia," Sodi says, quoting her mother and a common Italian proverb. "You don't age at the table." Enjoy the respite.

### Cook Ahead

Plan dishes that you can make the day before and then heat up in the oven or on the stovetop. Almost all soups and stews only improve overnight. Quiches, pies, roasted meats and sauces also do well. Most baked or refrigerated desserts can be prepared a day ahead and stored, or you can purchase a dessert from a bakery or grocery store.

Consider preparing a dessert in ramekins if you have a set at home so individual servings will be a breeze—but remember that cake and tart recipes will need less oven time in the small containers. Any other dishes should use recipes that can be partially prepared and finished with a simple step or two when guests arrive, like fish in parchment paper that can marinate ahead of time and then be finished in the oven, without keeping you in the kitchen for oversight.

### Choose Wine and Drinks

When choosing what beverages to serve, consider what might go well with your menu, what you like to drink yourself and what the group might enjoy. Think also about what kind of night this should be. Do you want a tequila-induced dance party or a sparkling water-supported business card exchange? Otherwise, wine is the standard libation for dinner parties.

A 750-milliliter bottle contains about five glasses of wine. You can usually bet on three glasses per guest (factoring in whether you're inviting teetotalers or heavy tipplers) plus some extra so you don't run out, which generally means counting around one bottle per person to be safe. Be sure water is on the table at dinner, and refill your guests' glasses frequently to keep them happy, healthy—and not too sloppy.

Generally, you'll want to start your guests off with a glass of something bubbly—it eases transitions and tends to put people in a festive mood. "Everyone should have a magnum of pét-nat at home ready to roll for their guests as they walk in," says Jorge Riera, wine director at Frenchette, referring to a double-sized bottle of sparkling pétillant naturelle. After that, you can progress to white or red wine with the dinner. Plan on serving the same kind throughout the dinner, saving your guests' wine for another occasion or in case your wine runs out—unless you've informed them of what kind of wine to bring ahead of time.

## BE A GOOD HOST

As host, your job is to help guests get acquainted and comfortable with each other. Get them chatting by including a tidbit about each person when you introduce them, and if two guests share a common interest, be sure to add that as well. Otherwise, an engaging detail about one of the guests—a recent trip, an exciting new job or any significant life event—will start the conversation. Beyond that, the best gift you can give your guests is to set the tone yourself by being relaxed and convivial, regardless of whatever disasters might have befallen you in the kitchen.

### Discourage Cell Phones

As a host or a guest, you'll want to minimize cell phone use, which can quickly draw you away from the group activity of dining and talking. Answering texts and phone calls during dinner sends the rude message that the present company in front of you is less important, but zero phone time is a nearly

## TIPS FOR HOSTS

Consider place cards for groups of eight or more, especially if not everyone knows each other. "Just think carefully about how to mix your guests well," cautions Mondadori Sartogo. Think also about the level of formality of your dinner. For a very casual evening, there's no need for place cards even with a large group.

Get guests' bags and coats out of the way and into a closet or bedroom immediately upon arrival, while asking guests either to store or open the wine they brought, and to take care of any flowers.

Offer something to drink or show guests the drink station you've set up when they arrive, making introductions before returning to the kitchen to finish preparing.

Think about serving dessert in the living room or another setting away from the table to help mix up the group and start new conversations, or encourage people to change places at the table. Serve coffee or a digestif to help wrap things up.

impossible expectation these days. If you must take a call or send some texts, try to leave the room.

Of course, there may be people who want to broadcast the beauty of the table settings or the

with shocking messages underneath, such as "Your neighbor is deeply in love with you," creating an instant game of show-and-tell. As host, it's also a good idea to tell an entertaining story to your guests

> "
> As host, it's also a good idea to tell an entertaining story to your guests to get the ball rolling and elicit more stories.

wonder of the host's entree plate to their social media followers. Jeremiah Tower, the celebrity chef who helped define California cuisine and authored the 2016 book "Table Manners," green-lights this kind of behavior only if everyone is on board. "I've had people stop me from eating because one person wants to photograph the food. I could stab them with a fork!" he sniffs, coming back to his essential rule: Think of others; don't upset anyone.

### Cue the Conversation

Conversation is vital to a successful dinner party— almost as much as food. The first step toward ensuring that your night holds some fascinating repartee is by inviting people you know enjoy making conversation or have interesting stories and opinions to share. If many of your guests don't know each other, or even if they do, the best way to warm up the atmosphere is to introduce an element of fun to the evening. At one dinner, Costanza Paravicini, whose namesake Milan atelier produces whimsical hand-painted plates, gave guests plates inscribed

to get the ball rolling and elicit more stories. Tales of childhood, zany early jobs or past shared experiences are the type of anecdotes that will help guests connect to each other and spur their own memories to keep stories coming.

Though you'll want to defuse any bitter fights, utterly restrained politeness is not going to make for the most revelatory discussions, either, so don't fear some difference in opinion. "The three things you're never supposed to talk about—sex, politics and religion—are the most interesting topics," says Tower, "so bring them up as long as it doesn't insult anyone, and you keep it fun and non-controversial"— unless controversy is what you want. Whatever topic you may introduce, if no one's following your conversational lead after a minute or two, put away those baby photos and wrap it up, he counsels.

# AFTER THE PARTY'S OVER

## CLEANUP

The jury's out on whether to take time away from your guests to wash dishes immediately after the meal or to leave them for the morning after and not abandon your post as the anchor of the dinner party. Getting at least some of them out of the way will make your morning much better, but it's undoubtedly easier if someone's helping you with the dinner and you can tag-team between guests and dish duty. At minimum, cork and store any extra wine, put away leftovers and get dishes soaking in the sink or a plastic tub.

## SAY "THANK YOU"

If your guests contributed to making the dinner a success—pulling off a surprise party or bringing over food, for example—be sure to send a thank-you note the next day. The format should be at least as formal as the invitation you sent.

Guests should always send a thank-you note to hosts—just look at all the preparation they went through to give you a lovely evening. Here also the format should at least match the type of invitation sent, but, when in doubt, sending a handwritten note or flowers is always greatly appreciated. Thank your host for what you enjoyed most about the evening. If you thought the meal was delicious or the dining room was beautiful, be sure to mention that, and add a note about getting together in the future.

# 3

# Invest

## SAVE · BUDGET · SPEND

**IF YOU'RE ANYTHING LIKE US,** this is probably the topic you dread most: dealing with your money.

There are so many things working against us when it comes to getting our finances in order: cultural taboos that make money difficult to talk about; no systemic education to teach how to be better at money; and the misguided way we equate personal wealth with personal worth.

Fixing your finances is never easy. But you have to start somewhere, and this chapter is just what you need.

**THIS CHAPTER WILL HELP YOU WITH ALL OF THAT AND MORE, AND WHEN YOU'RE FINISHED, YOU'LL KNOW HOW TO:**

- Start saving for retirement, or get better at saving if you've already started

- Get beyond the stigmas that prevent you from openly discussing money

- Find a professional adviser who can help you make better decisions

- Finally create a simple budget you'll stick to

- Save a couple of extra bucks this week

- And so much more

# How to Win at Retirement Savings

BY RON LIEBER

**WHILE MOST WORKERS ARE RESPONSIBLE** for their own retirement savings these days, high schools don't have required classes on 401(k)'s and Individual Retirement Accounts (IRAs). And colleges usually don't teach anything about Roth IRAs or 403(b)'s. That's where we come in. Here is what you need to know about saving for life after you stop working and about getting on the path toward a comfortable retirement, no matter your career or the size of your paycheck.

## START EARLY

The most important advice about saving for retirement is this: Start now. Why? Several reasons:

### The Magic of Compound Interest

You've probably read about this before, but the best way to understand it is to see it in front of you—and, as always, we're here to help. Check out the graph at the top of the next page.

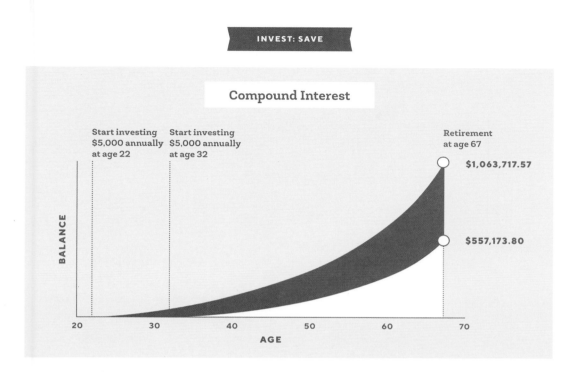

## Compound Interest

Start investing $5,000 annually at age 22

Start investing $5,000 annually at age 32

Retirement at age 67

$1,063,717.57

$557,173.80

BALANCE

AGE

20    30    40    50    60    70

Yes, we did that math correctly. If two people put the same amount of money away each year ($5,000), earn the same return on their investments (6 percent annually) and stop saving upon retirement at the same age (67), one will end up with nearly twice as much money just by starting at 22 instead of 32. Put another way: The investor who started saving 10 years earlier would have about $500,000 more at retirement. It's that simple.

### Saving Is a Habit

It may make rational, mathematical sense to start saving early, but it isn't always easy. But the instinct to save grows as you do it. It'll start to feel good as you see that account balance grow.

### How Much Should You Save?

The short answer: As much as you reasonably can, says Carl Richards, our Sketch Guy columnist.

Sure, you'll see articles telling you to save at least 15 percent of your income; that's a fine benchmark, though the true number will depend on how long you hope to work, what kind of inheritance you may get and a bunch of other unknowable facts. So start with something, even if it's just $25 per paycheck. Then, try to save a little bit more each year. Do it early and often enough so that saving becomes second nature.

## UNDERSTANDING YOUR INVESTMENT ACCOUNT OPTIONS

Now that you've made the right choice in deciding to save for retirement, make sure you are investing that money wisely.

The lineup of retirement accounts is a giant bowl of alphabet soup: 401(k)'s, 403(b)'s, 457s, IRAs, Roth IRAs, Solo 401(k)'s and all the rest. They came into existence over the decades for specific reasons, designed to help people who couldn't get all the benefits of the other accounts. But the result is a system that leaves many confused.

The first thing you need to know is that your account options will depend in large part on where and how you work.

## If You Work at a For-Profit Employer

If your for-profit employer offers any workplace retirement savings plan, it's probably a 401(k). (Many smaller employers do not.) You can generally sign up for this anytime (not just during your first week on the job or during specific periods each year). All you have to do is fill out a form saying what percentage of your paycheck you want to save, and your employer will deposit that amount with a company (like Fidelity or Vanguard) that will hold it for you. Here, automation is your friend. Some employers will automatically raise your savings rate each year, if you let them. And you should.

### Things to Know About a 401(k)

**Matching:** If you're really lucky, your employer will match some of your savings. It may match everything you save, up to 3 percent of your salary. Or it may put in 50 cents for every dollar you save, up to 6 percent of your salary. Whatever the offer is, do whatever you can to get all of that free money. It's like getting an instant raise, one that will pay you even more over time thanks to the compound interest we were talking about before.

**Caps:** How much can you put aside in a 401(k)? The federal government makes the call on this, and it often goes up a bit each year. For 2019, the limit for employee contributions to a 401(k) was set at $19,000, and the catch-up contribution limit for employees 50 years old or older was set at $6,000. You can find the latest numbers on IRS.gov.

**Taxes:** As with most other employer-based plans, when you save in a 401(k) you don't pay income taxes on the money you set aside, though you'll have to pay taxes when you eventually take out the money.

## If You Work at a Non-Profit Employer

If you work for the government or for a nonprofit institution like a school, religious organization or a charity, you likely have different options, including 401(k), 403(b) and 457 plans.

**What to Know About a 457 Plan:** These are a lot like 401(k)'s, so read the section above to understand them better.

**What to Know About a 403(b) Plan:** These frequently show up at nonprofits—401(k)'s are more rare here—and often get complicated and expensive. You may be encouraged (or forced) to put your money into an annuity instead of a mutual fund, which is what 401(k) plans invest in. (More on mutual funds later.) Annuities technically are insurance products, and they are very difficult even for professionals to decipher. Which brings us to the expensive part: They often have very high fees.

In some instances, especially if your employer is not matching your contribution, you may want to skip using 403(b)'s altogether and instead use the IRAs discussed below.

## If Your Employer Offers No Plan or You're Self-Employed

People who are setting up their own retirement accounts will usually be dealing with IRAs, available at financial-services firms like big banks and brokerages. Other options might include Roth IRA, SEP and Solo 401(k) plans.

### What to Know About IRAs

**Choosing Where to Start an IRA:** Ask the financial institution for a complete table of fees to see how they compare. How high are the fees to buy and sell your investments? Are there monthly account maintenance fees if your balance is too low?

In general, what you invest in tends to have far more impact on your long-term earnings than where you store the money, since most of these firms have pretty competitive account fees nowadays.

**Caps:** As with 401(k)'s, there may be limits to the amount you can deposit in an IRA each year, and the annual cap may depend on your income and other circumstances. The federal government will adjust the limits every year or two. You can see the latest numbers online.

**Taxes:** Perhaps the biggest difference between IRAs has to do with taxes. Depending on your income, you may be able to get a tax deduction for your contributions to a basic IRA up to a certain dollar amount each year. Again, check the up-to-date government information on income and deposit limits and ask the firm where you've opened the IRA for help. After you hit the tax-deductible limit, you may be able to put money into an IRA but you won't get any tax deduction. As with 401(k)'s, you'll pay taxes on the money once you withdraw it in retirement.

**What to Know About Roth IRAs:** The Roth IRA is a breed of IRA that behaves a little differently. With the Roth, you pay taxes on the money before you deposit it, so there's no tax deduction involved upfront. But once you do that, you never pay taxes again as long as you follow the normal withdrawal rules. Roth IRAs are an especially good deal for younger people with lower incomes who don't pay a lot of income taxes now. The federal government has strict income limits on these kinds of everyday contributions to a Roth. You can find those limits at IRS.gov.

**What Are SEPs and Solo 401(k)s?** Another variation on the IRA is a SEP (which is short for Simplified Employee Pension), and there is also a Solo 401(k) option for the self-employed. They come with their own set of rules that may allow you to save more than you could with a normal IRA.

**What happens if you change jobs?** When you leave an employer, you may choose to move your money out of your old 401(k) or 403(b) and combine it with other savings from other previous jobs. If that's the case, you'll generally do something called "rolling the money over" into an IRA. Brokerage firms offer a variety of tools to help you do that.

That said, some employers will try to talk you into leaving your old account under their care, while new employers may try to get you to roll your old account into their plan. Why do they do this? Because the more money they have in their accounts, the less they have to pay in fees to run the program for all employees.

## HOW TO INVEST YOUR MONEY

**You don't need to be financially savvy to make smart investment decisions.**

### DON'T GET FANCY

Dozens of books exist on the right way to invest. Tens of thousands of people spend their careers suggesting that they have the best formula. So let us try to cut to the chase with a simple formula that should help you do just fine as long as you save enough.

Think humble, boring, simple and cheap.

Humility comes first. Yes, there are people who can pick stocks or mutual funds (which are collections of stocks, bonds or both) that will do better than anyone else's picks. But it's impossible to predict who they are or whether the people who have done it in the past will do it again. And you, researching stocks or industries or national economies, are unlikely to outwit the markets on your own, part-time.

But leaving your money behind or rolling it into your new employer's plan may have disadvantages. Most employer plans may have only a limited menu of investments, but your IRA provider will generally let you invest in whatever cheap index funds you want.

Also, it's generally best to keep all of your retirement money in one place; it's easier to keep track of it that way. So, roll all your retirement accounts into an IRA once you leave a company to simplify things, especially as you near retirement. You can't

the same way you might if you owned Apple stock. But those big swings come with powerful feelings of greed, fear and regret, and those feelings may cause you to buy or sell your investments at the worst possible time. So, best to avoid the emotional tumult by touching your investments as little as possible.

## How to Choose Index Funds

How much of each kind of index fund should you have? They come in different flavors. Some try to

> *Roll all your retirement accounts into an IRA once you leave a company to simplify things, especially as you near retirement.*

count on former employers to keep in touch as your home or email addresses change. Nor will every entity that has an account in your name necessarily track you down when you near retirement.

## THE BORING GLORY OF INDEX FUNDS

Your best bet is to buy something called an index fund and keep it forever. Index funds buy every stock or bond in a particular category or market. The advantage is that you know you'll be capturing all of the returns available in, say, big American stocks or bonds in emerging markets.

And yes, buying index funds is boring. You usually won't see enormous day-to-day swings in prices

buy every stock in the United States, large or small, so that you have exposure to the entire American stock market in one package. Others try to buy every bond a company issues in a particular country. Some investment companies sell something called an exchange-traded fund (ETF), which are index funds that are easier to trade. Either flavor is fine, since you won't be buying or selling the funds much anyway.

As to your own allocation between, say, stock funds and bond funds, much will depend on your age and how much risk you're comfortable taking. Stock funds, for instance, tend to bounce around more than bond funds, and stocks in certain emerging markets tend to bounce around more than an index fund that owns, say, the stock of every big company in the United States (or every one on earth).

**Get Help:** Most employer-based plans, like 401(k)'s and even plenty of 403(b)'s, contain target-date mutual funds. These are baskets of funds that may contain some combination of stocks and bonds from different size companies from all over the world. You can choose one of these funds based on the year you hope to retire—the goal year will be in the name of the fund. So, if you're 40 years from retirement, you'd pick a fund with the year in the name that is closest to 40 years from now. Then, the fund slowly changes the mix of funds over time so it gets a bit less risky with each year, as you get closer to the period when you'll need the money.

**No Help Available?** If you're on your own, one option is to pick a single target-date fund made up entirely of index funds and just shovel all of your retirement savings into that. That way, you have all of your savings portioned into an appropriate mix that the fund manager will adjust as you get older (and presumably less tolerant of risky stocks).

Some companies called robo-advisers offer a different service. These robots will first ask you a series of questions to gauge your goals and risk tolerance. Then, they'll custom-craft a portfolio of cheap, indexed investments.

## FEES

Nothing in life is free, even when it comes to saving for retirement.

### The Downside of Retirement Accounts

Retirement accounts are not free, and the fees you pay eat into your returns, which can cost you plenty come retirement. If you are employed, the company that runs your plan (and whose name appears on the account statements) is charging your employer fees for the service. Plus each individual mutual fund in the plan has its own costs. If you are self-employed, you'll be charged for your IRA at the mutual fund level and then pay whatever fees (if any) that the brokerage firm levies on an annual basis or for each trade you make in your account.

Yet another reason to pick index funds: Index funds tend to be the cheapest investments available, in addition to doing quite well over time when compared to other funds run by people trying to outperform everyone else's market predictions. So investing in index funds is like winning twice.

If you want to learn more about identifying and deciphering retirement account fees, employees of large organizations should check out Brightscope .com, which rates thousands of employer-based plans.

If you're saving on your own and are curious about a particular target-date mutual fund and its fees, you can check its ranking on Morningstar.ca, a financial research firm, and compare it to other funds. As for those robo-advisers, the funds they'll put you in are usually quite cheap. You'll usually pay another quarter of a percentage point of your balance each year in exchange for their assistance in putting your portfolio together and keeping the

# ROUTINE FINANCIAL TUNE-UPS

Once you set them up, it only takes a few minutes a
year to keep tabs on your retirement accounts.

························································

After setting up automatic savings from your
paycheck, it's easy to forget about it. (And if you
do, that's OK. You'll likely be pleasantly surprised
when you do check in on your funds in a few
years.) But, if you can spare an hour every year to
check in on your accounts, you can ensure that
you're doing the best you can with your well-
earned money.

## TO DO

### Save 1 Percentage Point
### More from Your Paycheck
**TIME REQUIRED: 5 MINUTES**

If you followed our earlier advice, you set it up
so you have money automatically taken out of
each paycheck for your retirement account. You
barely miss it, right? So increasing your savings
by another percentage point probably won't hurt
your budget much. Over time, it could add up to
six figures in additional savings.

### Reconsider Your Investments
**TIME REQUIRED: 30 MINUTES**

Are you saving too much for a down payment
or children's college tuition but not enough for
retirement? The home may be able to wait, and
it's easier to borrow money for a child's education
than it is to get loans to pay for your retirement
expenses. Make sure you are investing wisely,
for the most important things.

### Rebalance Your Investments
**TIME REQUIRED: 30 MINUTES**

It's been a great half decade for stocks. So if you
set up accounts five years ago with the intent
of having 70 percent of your money in stocks,
the growth in those stocks may mean that your
investments are now in a stock allocation that's
many percentage points higher. If so, it's time to
sell some stock and buy, say, more bond mutual
funds to put things back into balance.

investments in their proper proportions. You can absolutely save that money by handling those trades on your own. But the question you have to ask yourself is whether you'll have the discipline to continue doing it year after year after year. If not, then that fee might seem like a reasonable price to pay for the help (and for keeping you from making bad trades).

### Fees Too High?

Don't like how high your fees are? You can try to lobby for better 401(k) or 403(b) plans.

## GETTING YOUR MONEY WHEN YOU NEED IT

### Before Retirement

**For a 401(k) Plan:** It's possible to get access to your money before you retire. Most 401(k) plans offer loans, where you can borrow from your investments. The good news: If you receive a loan from a 401(k) plan, you pay interest to yourself.

The bad news: You may miss out on market gains during the repayment period. If you leave an employer before you've paid off the loan, you have to repay in full quickly, lest the loan turn immediately into an official withdrawal.

If you want to withdraw money from a 401(k) plan permanently before the legal retirement age, it may be possible depending on your plan. Such withdrawals are generally known as hardships, and they have a special set of rules you can look up at IRS.gov.

**For an IRA:** With IRAs, you have to start taking a certain amount of money out each year once you turn 70½. That's the government's way of forcing you into converting that money into income that it can tax, even if you don't need the money right away. Roth IRAs, however, are not subject to the same withdrawal rules. If you're under 70, the early withdrawal rules require taxes and penalties, just as they do with a 401(k). But you can take some money out of some accounts for certain special-occasion purposes, like buying a home for the first time or paying college tuition. You can read more about the exceptions at IRS.gov.

### Once You're Retired

When the time comes to hang up the workboots, how much can and should you take out each year? For many years, financial professionals figured that if you took out no more than 4 percent of your savings each year starting at age 65 or so, you stood a very good chance of outliving your money. But so much depends on the nature of your investments, your age, your health, your spending and charity goals and a host of other things. Given that, following a universal rule of thumb could be dangerous.

That's why talking to a financial professional about your entire financial life as you approach retirement is probably a good idea. Make sure to speak to someone who agrees to act as a fiduciary, which means they pledge (see "Everything You Need to Know About Seeking Financial Advice" later in this section) to work in your best interest. If you're not seeking a long-term relationship, find a financial planner who is willing to work by the hour or on a flat-fee project basis.

## COMMON QUESTIONS
### What about Social Security?

Chances are, Social Security will still be around once you hit the eligibility age, but it probably won't provide enough money, after taxes, for all the expenses you'll face in retirement. Plus, it's possible that some of the rules will change before it's your turn to collect.

In general, if you can, you should wait until age 70 to take your Social Security money, since the monthly checks will be bigger at that point. So there may be a gap you need to bridge if you want or need to retire before you turn 70.

### If there are two adults in the family who both work, should they both be saving for retirement?

Yes. Two of the biggest potential expenses in retirement are health care and long-term care, like paying for a nursing home. You both may need above-average amounts of treatment and assistance, so more savings will mean more choices later on (and more tax breaks at present if you do save).

### How do I know if I'm saving enough?

You can't, really. It's hard to know how long you'll want to work, how long you'll be physically able to work, how long an employer or customers will be willing to let you work for them, how much money you'll actually want to spend once you retire, and how long you'll live when you're done working. Plus, you can't predict your investment returns.

Given all the variables, you may be tempted to throw up your hands and put off the decision to start saving or to increase your savings. Please don't.

**Before you pay anyone for financial help, do some careful work (with your partner, if relevant) and consider the following:**

What do you value most in life?

How can spending and giving support those values?

How much is enough when it comes to housing, travel and leisure?

How much is too much?

--------------------------------------------

*Better yet, start thinking about those questions decades before retirement. The sooner your start, the calmer you'll probably be about the money you do save and the more resolute you'll be about putting enough aside to meet all your lifelong goals.*

If the possibilities feel overwhelming, just save as much as you reasonably can, as our Sketch Guy columnist, Carl Richards, puts it. Again, more savings now will mean more and better options later.

## This is hard. How do I find a financial adviser who can help?

The standard advice is to talk to someone you trust and see whom they use and like. But plenty of smart people know very little about money and have no idea if a financial adviser is treating them poorly.

**Check Their Certifications:** If an adviser is a certified financial planner (CFP) or chartered financial analyst (CFA), that means that he or she has learned a lot along the way and passed some difficult exams to earn those initials. (Other titles and acronyms may mean much less.)

**Then Set Up an Initial Meeting with a Few Advisers:** Ask each if he or she pledges to act in your best interest, always. The fancy term for this is acting as a "fiduciary," and by all means ask your adviser to take the fiduciary pledge we created a few years back. (See "Everything You Need to Know About Seeking Financial Advice" later in this section for a sample of the fiduciary pledge.)

Then, ask a potential adviser questions about the fees you'll be paying—to the adviser, for your investments and anything else.

**Finally, Compare Your Notes About Each Adviser You Spoke To:** Be real about how real you're going to need to get with this stranger. So much of these money conversations are about feelings: our fears, our goals and our strongest values expressed through our spending, saving and giving. Does this person care about your feelings? Are the people you're talking to even asking about them? If not, keep looking.

## FINANCIAL ADVISER ORGANIZATIONS

Two good places to start the hunt for an adviser are the **National Association of Personal Financial Advisors (NAPFA)** and the **Garrett Planning Network**. Members of both organizations tend to be transparent about their fees. Sure, there are some bad seeds in these two groups (as there are everywhere), and there are plenty of great advisers who work for more traditional brokerage firms (who are not members of the two groups). But your odds of quickly finding someone good will be high in these two organizations.

# We're All Afraid to Talk About Money. Here's How to Break the Taboo.

BY KRISTIN WONG

**"I WANT TO GET MY OWN PLACE.** How much is your rent?" a friend once asked. He immediately put his hand over his mouth.

"Sorry," he said. "That's so rude."

Many of us grow up learning that money is one of a few topics—like politics, sex and religion—that you should avoid in polite company. You don't brag about your net worth. You don't share your salary with colleagues. You try not to ask your friends about their rent, even if it helps put your budget in perspective.

We're discouraged from talking about money at every turn, but if you want to fix your financial situation, talking about it is necessary.

Even setting aside that social taboo of discussing money, there are practical hurdles in your way to getting better at money: Learning about money is intimidating, and there's no structural system in place to teach us. Further still, we look at poor money skills as something to be ashamed and embarrassed of, which can keep us from being honest about money and seeking out the right kind of help.

"It's difficult for people to discuss money because there's no real agreed-upon standard of measurement for financial metrics," said Shannon McLay, a former financial adviser who left Merrill Lynch to launch The Financial Gym, a financial planning firm in Manhattan.

"We all know physical health numbers, like BMI, weight and clothing sizes, so we can assess where we fall on that spectrum," Ms. McLay said. "Because of a lack of agreed-upon financial metrics, people feel fear or shame around what their finances look like."

All of these forces—the social taboo, the intimidation factor, embarrassment—conspire to keep us from talking about money and improving our circumstances. For example, according to data from Fidelity Investments, 43 percent of Americans don't know how much money their spouse makes, yet fighting about money is a top predictor of divorce. When you don't even know your household income, you can pretty much guarantee a financial fight will eventually erupt.

"There are few things that can cause joy, shame, contentment, anxiety and stress the way that money does," said Korrena Bailie, a financial journalist and senior editor of personal finance at The Wirecutter, a *New York Times* company that reviews and recommends products.

"If your finances cause you stress and anxiety, it's natural to want to keep this to yourself because you might feel embarrassed or ashamed about the decisions you made," she said.

Ms. McLay added: "When you ignore your financial situation, minor problems happening on a regular basis build up to very substantial challenges."

It's time we all change the story and open up about money.

Break the silence. It's hard to learn about something when you're discouraged from talking about it. In that way, silence becomes a tool for oppression.

Student loan servicer Navient, for example, has been sued for misleading borrowers about repayment options, collectively costing those borrowers as much as $4 billion in interest. Wells Fargo made headlines for secretly opening millions of fraudulent customer accounts that generated at least $2.6 million in fees. If you don't pay attention to your finances, there's always someone waiting to take advantage of that fact.

As wages continue to stagnate and the income gap continues to widen, talking and learning about money is crucial for change.

"Not talking about money can have sweeping social effects, like stopping women from getting equal pay for equal work in the workplace," Ms. Bailie said. This issue came up in 2018 with Google in the spotlight. The Department of Labor lawsuit and investigation against the company claimed that "discrimination against women in Google is quite extreme, even in this industry." Google refused to disclose data about employee salary history, according to the suit.

OK, so you're convinced: Talking about money is important. So how do we begin?

## START SMALL

If you're intimidated by personal finance and unsure of where to start, remember that you don't have to learn everything about money at once.

Start with one financial lesson at a time. If you have a hard time saving, focus your literacy on emergency funds. If you want to get out of debt, research different debt payoff methods. Read a money blog or listen to a money podcast during your work commute. Dedicate just half an hour to financial literacy a day, and you'll be surprised at how much you learn over time.

## TALK TO YOUR FRIENDS

"I think that speaking with friends about your financial situation is critical for breaking the taboo around money," Ms. McLay said. The more comfortable you are talking openly among your peers about topics like retirement plans, student loans and budgeting, the more opportunity you have to learn from each other.

"The more we talk about our situations and either accept them or work on improving them, the healthier our relationship with money will get," she said.

## BE MORE HONEST ABOUT MONEY

Let's say you want to throw a little extra at your student loan this month, which might mean cutting back on restaurants. When your friends invite you out for sushi, it's easy to skirt the issue with an excuse like, "I'm busy that night, I need to do laundry." Try being honest about where you stand with your finances instead.

This also creates the possibility for learning. Maybe your friend tells you how she paid off her loan early, for example. Or maybe she just starts suggesting cheaper hangout alternatives. Either way, you invite better financial habits and solutions when you break the money taboo.

## FIND LIKE-MINDED PEOPLE

When you're trying to get more comfortable with money, it helps to surround yourself with people who are on the same page, who have similar goals and are open to talking about those goals. You can use Facebook or LinkedIn to search for local money meetup groups.

There are also online forums and communities, like Ladies Get Paid, Mr. Money Mustache, Rockstar

## SET A GOAL

Having a plan for your money may be the best way to get comfortable with it. Ms. McLay said the most successful clients she's had are the ones who have clearly defined goals for themselves.

"Set three to four financial goals, like saving $5,000 or making $45,000 a year in a job, and start working toward those goals," she said. "The more financial goals you achieve, the more comfortable you'll get with your financial situation."

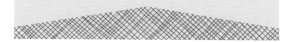

Finance, Reddit Personal Finance or Bogleheads, where members share negotiation tactics, debt payoff strategies and other important money moves.

"There are very few financial problems that improve by ignoring or neglecting them," Ms. Bailie added. "When you begin to understand the value of being open and transparent about money, it starts to feel like an imperative."

# Everything You Need to Know About Seeking Financial Advice

BY TARA SIEGEL BERNARD

**MANY PEOPLE TURN TO A PROFESSIONAL FOR FINANCIAL ADVICE** when they have a big problem to solve: How much do I need to save for my children's college? Can I afford the bigger house? Will I run out of money in retirement?

The answers to these questions could vary—widely—depending on the type of financial adviser you work with. If you find yourself sitting across from an annuity sales agent, for example, chances are that person will find some way to justify an annuity. And that may not be the right solution.

All of this means that the onus remains on savers to ensure the professional they choose is the right one.

Here are several questions to ask yourself when considering paying for financial advice.

## WHAT KIND OF ADVISER SHOULD I WORK WITH?

If you're thinking about hiring a financial planner, read this primer first.

You'll want to hire the type of financial adviser who promises to act as a fiduciary all of the time, with all of your money, which is a fancy way of saying that person must be loyal to you first. In fact, you should ask your financial planner to sign a fiduciary pledge, a promise not to profit at your expense.

Investment advisers, who generally must register with the SEC or a state securities regulator, must work in their clients' best interest, regardless of what accounts they are working with.

But being a "registered investment adviser" alone doesn't qualify a professional to answer your most challenging money questions. You also need to check that person's educational background and training. Certified financial planners, for example, must satisfy some of the more rigorous curriculum and experience requirements. Chartered financial consultants undergo something similar.

Brokers, who may call themselves advisers, don't necessarily carry any of these credentials. Instead, they may simply pass licensing exams that permit them to sell certain investments. Outside of your retirement money, they are required only to recommend products that are "suitable," which isn't necessarily the best or most cost-effective. And why should you settle for less?

## HOW MUCH ADVICE DO I NEED?

If you want to get started saving—or make sure you're on track to meet certain goals—you may want to pay a financial adviser for a financial plan (which could cost somewhere in the neighborhood of $1,200 in New York). Otherwise, you may want to pay a planner by the hour—or some other flat-fee arrangement—for time and advice.

People who want to hand over the reins of their portfolio to be managed by a professional may pay a percentage of their assets, typically around 1 percent.

The key is to find an adviser who does not get compensated only if that person sells you something.

## WHAT IF I DON'T WANT A FULL-TIME HUMAN ADVISER?

Check out the robo-advisers or hybrid services that use human planners who rely heavily on technology. They typically charge just a fraction of what a full-time human money manager costs.

## WHAT IF I NEED ADVICE ABOUT INSURANCE OR ANNUITIES?

This is a tricky area where a lot of people get talked into buying products they don't really need. If you want to buy life insurance, you might pay a financial planner, for example, for a couple of hours to analyze what's appropriate for your situation.

Then, you can seek out a sales agent with access to policies from several providers or buy a policy through online brokerages like PolicyGenius or AccuQuote. This is especially important as employers are increasingly pushing the onus of disability insurance onto their employees.

## WHERE CAN I START MY SEARCH?

Peruse the Garrett Planning Network, the National Association of Personal Financial Advisors and XY Planning Network for someone with expertise working with people like you.

And be sure to check their history for any black marks. Try the Investment Adviser Public Disclosure website. It scans data from the Securities and Exchange Commission, as well as BrokerCheck and state securities regulators' sites.

# THE FIDUCIARY PLEDGE

We've written a version of the pledge that you can use the next time you're shopping for an adviser:

I, the undersigned, pledge to exercise my best efforts to always act in good faith and in the best interests of my client, _____ , and will act as a fiduciary. I will provide written disclosure, in advance, of any conflicts of interest that could reasonably compromise the impartiality of my advice. Moreover, in advance, I will disclose any and all fees I will receive as a result of this transaction and I will disclose any and all fees I pay to others for referring this client transaction to me. This pledge covers all services provided.

Signed _____

Date _____

# Stop Wasting Money and Finally Start a Budget

BY TIM HERRERA

**DIETS AND BUDGETS HAVE ONE IMPORTANT THING** in common: The best one is the one you'll stick with.

And that's pretty much it! There's really no wrong way to make and maintain a budget as long as you're tracking your spending versus your income and accounting for where every dollar goes. It's a simple idea, but it's one that can be difficult to pull off. Still, it's an exercise in financial responsibility that you'll benefit from no matter what your income is.

Only around 40 percent of Americans use a budget, but for those who do, the benefits can be huge. Budgeting can help you find sources of income leak (those habits you don't really think about but that can drain your bank account), it can put you on a path toward saving for things like an emergency fund or home down payment, and it can boost your retirement savings, among many other benefits.

There are tons of apps and websites to help you create a budget, but experts say the best way to manage your money is to do it yourself by writing down everything: Doing so gives you complete ownership of your financial decisions, and it drives home the importance of understanding where every dollar goes.

If you've never created a budget or if you need a refresher, the simplest way to get going is to write down every single expense in a given month, then break them down into two categories: **fixed expenses** (the things you must pay, like rent, bills and loan payments) and **discretionary expenses** (things you control, like food, entertainment, car-related expenses and clothes).

You have many possible routes to take from there, but a good rule of thumb often suggested is to get your overall spending to fit into the 50-30-20 method: 50 percent of your post-tax income should go to those fixed expenses; 20 percent should go to long-term savings like a 401(k) or a Roth IRA; and the rest should go to your discretionary spending. The exact proportions will vary person to person, but that general budget makeup is a good mix to aim for.

If you'd rather use an app or a service to track your budget and expenses, The Wirecutter, a *New York Times* company that reviews and recommends products, suggests You Need a Budget for most people. This web and mobile app guides you through the process of creating a budget and itemizing your expenses, and it gives feedback about your spending habits. (Its biggest flaw, however, is that it'll cost you a little more than $80 a year to use, so if you go this route, make sure you're adding at least that much in increased savings by using it.) Other options are Simple and Mint.

Just remember: The best budget is the one you'll stick with.

## THE 50-30-20 BUDGET

This is a simple, effective way to allocate your post-tax income. It splits your spending into three categories:

**Fixed expenses:**
Rent, bills and loan repayment

**Discretionary expenses:**
Food, clothing and entertainment

**Long-term savings:**
401(k) or Roth IRA

Put this portion toward **long-term savings.**

20%

50%

30%

Around a third should go to **discretionary spending.**

Spend roughly half of your post-tax income on **fixed expenses.**

# What is the worst money decision you've ever made?

After my husband and I got married, we hired a financial planner to manage our investments. We'd have quarterly meetings with her, but I wasn't looking under the hood. I launched my podcast around that time, and my first guest was Tony Robbins, who talked to me a lot about fees. He was saying, You think you're doing so well because you have this beautiful, diversified, asset-allocated portfolio, but do you know how much that costs in terms of the management fee? It may be a small percentage difference, but if you've invested thousands of dollars for the next 30 years, that can be tens of thousands in fees. I emailed our planner to send me the expense ratios for all our funds, and there were a handful of funds that qualified as too expensive, i.e., over 1.5 percent. Some she justified; others we got rid of. Eventually, we gave up having a planner entirely. She'd set things up, giving us big-picture guidance, and now it was time to do it ourselves.

— **Farnoosh Torabi,** creator and host of the "So Money" podcast, and author of *When She Makes More*

My first job was at a personal finance magazine, so on the advice of my very smart co-workers, I started contributing to a 401(k) right away. But until the end of 2018, I still hadn't opened a Roth IRA, which is a favorite financial account of many financial writers. Though I knew I *should* open one, I didn't at first because I figured the 401(k) was good enough. Then I wrote an article going in depth on Roths, and I realized it is a better vehicle for a lot of people, especially for younger people. With the traditional workplace 401(k), you're getting a predetermined set of funds and things you can invest in, and sometimes the fees are higher. With a Roth, there are more options, and since you're contributing money you've already been taxed on, you don't pay taxes on the money or the earnings when you take them out, and you can take out your contributions anytime. There are a few rules and restrictions, of course, but it's a lot more flexible than 401(k)s or traditional IRAs, and it's probably a better deal for a lot of people. I write about the benefits all the time, and I even tell my friends to open one, but it took around three years to actually invest money in one and check it off my to-do list. It was just this weird mental block I had.

— **Alicia Adamczyk,** personal finance writer at the website Lifehacker

# You Need a Raise. How Do You Start the Conversation?

BY KRISTIN WONG

**IT'S PERSONAL FINANCE 101:** If you want to be good with money, you have to learn how to save it. But there are only so many slices of avocado toast you can refuse. At some point, being good with money requires something a bit more difficult: earning more of it.

As awkward as the conversation can be, making more money often means asking for more money. But for many of us, the idea of asking for a raise is unimaginably awkward. It feels audacious and greedy, like you might as well be asking for a kidney or firstborn child.

"I recommend that people ask for a raise at least once a year, as part of an annual review," said Devon Smiley, a negotiation consultant.

Some employers offer regular cost-of-living raises, but the economy has thrown a wrench in the concept of the traditional salary review.

"But that doesn't mean you're limited to that opportunity to discuss your salary and seek an adjustment," Ms. Smiley said.

Consider this: Yes, you're asking for more money, but you're also bringing value to your company. Ideally, you're making them more profitable in your own way, with your own unique set of skills. If you're not sure how much to ask for, use sites like Glassdoor.com or Payscale.com to research how much your skills and role command, on average.

## FOLLOW BEHIND BIG WINS

If you've recently scored a big work accomplishment or finished a successful project, use that milestone to make the case for your raise.

"You want to enter a salary negotiation on a high note, with indisputable evidence of the value you're contributing to the company," Ms. Smiley said. Evidence is important. If you're overdue for a raise, simply asking might be all you need to do, but it can't hurt to be prepared.

"For example, instead of saying that you had 'great success in the new product launch,' try 'the launch exceeded target by 10 percent, bringing in 1,000 new customers,'" Ms. Smiley said. Think about the situation from your boss's perspective. Quantifiable evidence makes it easier for them to approach the higher-ups and ask for an increase, based on value.

However, gender can play a significant role in these discussions. Dr. Alice Stuhlmacher, chair of DePaul University's psychology department, has found that women often pay a social penalty when they negotiate. That is to say, women may be viewed as unlikable when they ask for a raise.

"Women should be extra prepared with documentation and comparison information," she said.

"Our general expectation for women is to be nice and put others' needs before their own," Dr. Stuhlmacher said. In other words, women aren't expected to be assertive, which makes negotiation tricky. While organizations should ultimately own this issue, Dr. Stuhlmacher said, there are some tactics that women might find especially helpful. "Some find it helpful to have a champion, involving others to help advocate for them," she added.

## TIMING IS IMPORTANT

Don't drop the question on your boss in passing. Ask to schedule a meeting during which you can sit down and talk specifically, and only, about salary. Ms. Smiley recommends an in-person conversation rather than via email or over the phone, but be mindful of your work dynamic. If you're a freelancer who works remotely a thousand miles away, asking for a phone meeting will have to suffice. Either way, try to schedule that meeting at least two weeks in advance, which gives both parties time to prepare.

Ms. Smiley suggested a quick script you can use when you ask for a meeting: "I'd like to meet to discuss my performance, contribution and compensation." Use your own words, of course, depending on your relationship with your employer, but be specific in your invite and mention you'd like to talk about salary so your request doesn't come as an uncomfortable surprise.

## CONSIDER BUDGET CYCLES

"Even though discussions may not happen until April, for example, those budgets have been decided months earlier, and that is when you need to start laying the groundwork for your raise," Ms. Smiley said. This gives your boss a head start so they have time to go to bat for you with the finance department. You can talk to your direct manager or HR department about your company's budget cycle, but it's probably a better idea to ask colleagues who have been with the company for a while.

"They're likely to know if the process is as perfectly mapped as the corporate flow chart would have you believe, or if there's an unofficial timetable that emerges instead," Ms. Smiley said.

## AVOID APOLOGETIC LANGUAGE

Another hurdle is psyching yourself up to ask. If you're afraid to ask for a raise, you're likely to start the conversation with something like, "I'm so sorry to bother you," or, "I know budgets are tight right now." Again, from your employer's perspective, it's not about you. It's about the value you bring to the table, so focus on that.

"Asking for a salary increase based on your achievements is nothing to be sorry about," Ms. Smiley said. "And if you lead with an excuse, don't be surprised when it comes right back at you along with a 'no.'"

## KNOW WHAT YOU'RE GOING TO SAY—AND HOW YOU'LL SAY IT

Here's another script to start the conversation: "Thanks so much for taking the time to meet with me, I appreciate it. I'd like us to discuss my performance in the role, the contributions I've made so far, and how that positions me in terms of salary and opportunity here at The Company."

This dialogue is polite and straightforward. You also want to show you're engaged, Ms. Smiley said. Try something like: "I'm really enjoying my work. Leading the Big Win Project was especially rewarding."

From there, go in for the ask. If you're looking for a raise to match a new or enhanced role at your company, here's what you can say: "Taking into consideration my experience and the responsibilities of this position, my salary expectation is X dollars." If you're simply asking for a raise in your current role, this will do: "Based on my successful track record in this role, I'm requesting a salary lift of X percent."

Again, speaking up can often be more difficult for women or people who aren't socialized to be assertive. In that case, it can't hurt to practice.

"One recommendation is building negotiation experience and training," Dr. Stuhlmacher said. "Practicing in low stakes situations can build confidence." This might mean calling a bill provider and haggling a lower rate, or speaking up when you want a different table at a restaurant. Get comfortable asking for small things, which will make it easier to ask for something big, like a raise.

## HAVE A BACKUP PLAN

If you get a no, you can try to ask for other benefits, like more time off, bonuses or the option to work more remotely. Better yet, ask what skills you can develop within the next few months to achieve that raise "and then do the work," Ms. Smiley said.

"And make sure you book another review in six months to discuss progress and compensation." Set the expectation that once you further develop these skills, it will be time to revisit the compensation conversation.

Remember, this can be a difficult conversation to have. If you feel greedy or self-conscious asking for more, it can make it easier to focus on the broader impact that your raise can have. "For your family, your community, for charities you support," Ms. Smiley said. "It's not just about fattening your bank account."

# Navigating the Financial Side of a Relationship

## BY MARIA TERESA HART

**COUPLES CAN FIGHT ABOUT ANYTHING;** it's just a fact of relationships. But arguments about money have a tendency to be particularly toxic, since they're layered with deep emotional and personal history.

In fact, researchers have shown there's a direct relationship between the number of times a couple has argued about their budget per month and their divorce rate.

Despite this, or maybe because of it, people tend to avoid financial talks with their partner. While standard marital advice has us studiously marking out "date nights" on the calendar to keep passion alive, there's no phrase for scheduling nights to preserve fiscal harmony.

I wanted to skirt that pitfall. Once a month, I have a calendar reminder pop up. It reads: "HOTTALK DOLLARDOLLAR BILLS Y'ALL." (Yes, in all caps.)

This is a little over-the-top and ridiculous. But injecting some levity into what can be a heated and emotional discussion—one where we lay our bank accounts bare—has allowed my husband and me to laugh a bit while tackling one of the most important conversations couples can have.

These chats do have their challenges, but they can also be deeply bonding. And more important, they can keep serious money problems at bay and help us save and invest more smartly. Here's how to start up your own financial date night with your partner.

## DIG INTO YOUR HISTORY

Your attitude about money begins in childhood, starting with your parents' behavior around spending and saving, experts say.

"Your first money memories were created when you understood money was more than just a toy," said Suze Orman, the financial expert and author of "The Money Class." After that moment, your attitude became shaped by a series of firsts, including your first allowance, first paycheck, first big-ticket purchase, first major money loss and so on. Analyzing this history is a key step in achieving financial harmony with another person.

These early memories are our "underlying blueprint," she said. Benjamin Seaman, a couples therapist and co-founder of the New York Center for Emotionally Focused Therapy, said that "unpacking the origins of our approach to money" leads to a deeper understanding on both sides and "an appreciation of people's raw spots."

In other words, just as you exchanged your romantic history with your partner, share your backstory when it comes to money.

## DON'T WITHHOLD INFORMATION

Money is an intimate subject, and we're coached from an early age to be secretive about it. It's hard to break that habit and let someone else in, and inviting another person into your pocketbook can mean risking judgment. ("You spend how much on avocado toast?!")

Revealing your finances also means losing some autonomy. Many of us see our bank balance as the ultimate achievement of independence. Mr. Seaman acknowledges this and sums up those feelings as: "Finally! I get to do what I want. I don't have my parents telling me what to do anymore." It's the freedom of impulse purchases and ice cream for dinner when no one else is watching.

But while sharing this information may make you vulnerable and accountable, you'll also gain a new openness in your relationship.

"You have to stand in the truth with your financial partner," Ms. Orman said. "You have to have the overarching goal of honesty and integrity."

## FACE THE HARDEST THINGS HEAD-ON

Consider financial date nights the moment to unburden yourself. In these discussions, "fear, shame and anger are the three internal obstacles," Ms. Orman said.

Mr. Seaman added that these feelings can multiply, leading to "cycles of shame and spending." (Picture a closet full of unused Amazon purchases or an online poker habit.) But voicing that burden, and being met with acceptance and love from your partner, can put you on the path to healing.

If you're on the receiving end of a confession from your partner, remember that having a common enemy is incredibly bonding. Teaming up to face something like student loan debt together can unite you, and these financial date nights give you the opportunity to be in the trenches together.

# KEEP IT LIGHT AND LAUGH ABOUT IT

There's a reason my calendar reminder doesn't say, "Reoccurring Money Talk With Husband," which sounds so crushingly serious. A little sprinkling of silly can keep your spirits up, even if your numbers are down.

## ADD HUMOR

Invite in humor anywhere you can, including account nicknames with personal jokes or spreadsheets with silly line items. (Our Hawaii honeymoon budget had an entry for "shark repellent.") The goal isn't to avoid hard subjects, but to dodge the hostility that could surround them. And if you're laughing, you're already defusing any potential anger.

## MAKE IT A DATE

But apart from humor, habits expert and best-selling author Gretchen Rubin said, it also helps to "be mindful about shaping the experience to make it as pleasant as possible." She suggested pairing your financial date nights with a special coffee drink or time outside on a nice day. Ms. Orman has her own approach, scheduling her financial check-ins with her wife on a relaxing Saturday night over a glass of wine. Make the setting and the associations positive, so when that calendar reminder pops up again, you're thinking, "Great!" not "Unsubscribe."

## REMEMBER THAT SOLUTIONS AREN'T UNIVERSAL

If you've found a system that works for you—like using only cash for purchases, money-tracking apps or a swear jar—don't assume it will work for your spouse.

Ms. Rubin believes you should avoid the mentality that "if your spouse would just do it the way you did it, then problem solved." Some of the deepest discords can occur when you shoehorn your approach onto your partner.

In her 2017 book, "The Four Tendencies," Ms. Rubin identified several character traits that shape people's habits and perspectives.

One of the trickiest is the "rebels," who want to buck the rules. While rebels won't respond well to Excel spreadsheets and budgeting mandates, they can get on board with other approaches.

"Rebels like a challenge," Ms. Rubin said. "They like to do things in unconventional ways. You could say to them: 'Let's do something crazy! Let's try to spend $10 a day for the next three months!'" and they will eagerly get on board.

Another personality group, "questioners" need to do their own research before committing. Before signing up for a 401(k), for instance, a questioner might want to see a chart showing the compound interest the account would earn.

"Obligers" seek outer accountability, so framing a financial step as a way to set a positive example for their children could motivate them. Give your partner room to zero in on his or her own approach to your shared goals.

## TAKE TIME TO DREAM

A budget can seem like drudgery: a forced diet on your spending buffet. But budgets aren't just about reining in your wallet; they're also about deciding where your money will go, road maps to shared destinations.

For this reason, financial date nights should include a discussion about the dreams you'd like to realize with your income.

"You should talk about your financial future," Ms. Orman said. A European getaway? A three-bedroom house? A pair of matching hoverboards? These are all dreams you can save toward.

Regular check-ins with your partner will keep you both excited and focused on those goals, and, if you want to get creative, you can even bring a little arts and crafts into it.

"I'm a big fan of vision boards and making things real any way you can," Mr. Seaman said. "When you put a little time into creating a goal chart or vision board, you're telling yourself, 'I believe in this.'" And you're giving that message to your partner, too.

# Why You Should Tell Your Co-workers How Much Money You Make

BY TIM HERRERA

## SO HOW MUCH DO YOU MAKE?

It's a loaded, deeply personal and often uncomfortable question. Along with our weight and age, our salary is a number to which we've assigned almost incomparable value.

And when we're asked, what many of us really hear is this: What's your worth as a person?

"Money is so tied up with really complex and difficult emotions, like shame, success, fear of failure and how people view you," said Brianna McGurran, a money expert at the personal finance blog NerdWallet. "So when you're talking about how much you earn, or how much you're saving, a lot of people end up tying that to their self-worth."

She added: "Salary is so close to our identity. It's the core part of all of this."

That money—along with sex, politics and religion—is a topic best avoided in polite conversation is a cultural concept many of us are raised on, and taboos around discussing income can be particularly sensitive.

But unlike not disclosing what's in your savings account or your 401(k), there are direct, concrete consequences for falling victim to salary secrecy, including wage suppression and a lack of transparency around pay inequity, which disproportionately affects women and minorities.

"Let's face it, it's 2018 and there's still serious disparities in pay based on race and gender," said Angela Cornell, the director of the Labor Law Clinic at Cornell Law School.

"So policies that discourage or prohibit employees from discussing these are problematic not just because of the National Labor Relations Act's clear prohibition," she said, "but also because they can make it difficult for employees in the private sector to learn that there are unlawful disparities."

## YES, IT'S OK—AND PERFECTLY LEGAL—TO TALK ABOUT IT

What many workers don't realize is that it is unlawful for private sector employers to prohibit employees from discussing wages and compensation, and it has been since the National Labor Relations Act was passed in 1935. (There are exceptions, including for supervisors, agriculture workers and domestic employees.)

Open discussion of salaries among peers and co-workers, experts said, is a powerful tool to fight pay inequity. Not only does it serve both selfish and altruistic means—it simultaneously puts you and your co-workers in a better position during salary negotiations—but pay transparency can even protect companies by "minimizing the risk of disparate treatment claims and increasing job satisfaction for workers," Ms. Cornell said.

Still, prohibiting or discouraging workers from openly discussing salaries, whether codified or implicitly built into a company's culture, is somewhat commonplace in workplaces.

"It's been the law of the land for many years that employers can't have policies or practices [that] discipline employees for discussing wages," Ms. Cornell said. "But that doesn't mean it hasn't been a common practice."

Horror stories of employees facing punishment for sharing salaries aren't difficult to dig up.

Elizabeth, who requested her last name not be used because of the sensitivity of discussing her salary, worked in sales at an arts company and this year shared her salary with a junior co-worker who was up for a promotion. That co-worker, during her own salary negotiation, let slip to a manager that Elizabeth had shared her salary.

"I got a call on my work phone to come to the board room," Elizabeth said. Her manager was there—"it was very dramatic, with the lights off"—and she told Elizabeth she wasn't allowed to share her salary, and she was creating a "bad environment," Elizabeth said.

Knowing that she was legally in the right, Elizabeth brushed off the encounter, and 10 minutes later her manager rushed over to apologize.

"She had gotten reprimanded herself from our HR department," Elizabeth said. Still, that experience was a major factor in Elizabeth's decision to leave the company a few months later.

Even the savviest among us can get caught up in the pressures of salary secrecy.

"I can remember in the not-too-distant past having been discouraged from talking about wages," Ms. Cornell said. She added that years ago she learned through a conversation about salaries with a male co-worker that he was making about $50,000 more than she was, and that there was "no objective justification for the disparity in pay, but he had been in the position for a longer period of time."

"That is not a good thing," she said. "It can lead to low morale, and there was no objective justification about the disparity in pay."

Kristin Wong, author of "Get Money: Live the Life You Want, Not Just the Life You Can Afford" and a personal finance contributor for *The New York Times*, recalls when she was reprimanded for discussing her salary with a co-worker:

After a few months on the job, my friend whispered that she'd received a small raise. Armed with this knowledge, I politely made the case for my own, without mentioning anything but my work ethic and commitment. My boss relented, but reprimanded me in the process.

"This is why I don't like my employees talking about money," she said.

You don't have to read too hard between the lines to grasp the real meaning: Employers can get away with paying workers less when those workers don't talk about money.

## CHANGING TIDES

In just the past few years, cultural norms and legislation have begun to unravel some of the forces that discourage open salary discussion, sometimes even tilting pay negotiations in favor of employees.

A handful of states, including California, Connecticut and Massachusetts, have banned employers from asking job candidates for a salary history, which shifts some leveraging power back to candidates. In 2014, President Barack Obama signed an executive order "prohibiting federal contractors from retaliating against employees who choose to discuss their compensation." And in some industries, including the news media, unionization has become a powerful force in fighting for worker wages.

Evan, a social media strategist in Atlanta who also requested his last name not be used, knows firsthand the benefits of open salary discussions.

After interviewing for jobs at competing marketing agencies last year, he realized he was being paid below the market rate for someone at his experience level. He told co-workers his discovery, and he said many of them were in the same situation.

"Eventually rumors started flying about: 'Hey, this person said this to leadership; this person is also complaining about it,'" he said.

After initially responding with halfhearted gestures and speeches about workplace culture, Evan said, leadership at the agency eventually succumbed to the pressure and gave every employee a raise.

"People got what they wanted," he said.

Jill Duffy, a writer, said for years she has been open about sharing her salaries and that she has been able to use that knowledge to "negotiate raises because of the information I got."

"I went in feeling confident about my worth and my value and what the company could afford to pay me," she said.

Other times, Ms. Duffy said, having that information is "just sort of confirming suspicions" that a company can afford to pay more than it currently is.

# THE BEST APPROACH: WIN-WIN

Having these conversations is much easier said than done,
but there are ways to gain confidence in discussing your salary.

Most important, Ms. McGurran said, is to be open and genuine, framing these conversations as beneficial for everyone involved. She suggests starting with people who are more senior than you, "maybe someone who has helped bring you on, or a previous manager, or someone who you really trust and wants to see you succeed." This can give you a bigger-picture view of your company's salaries.

From there, try to approach peers, co-workers or fellow alumni in off-campus, laid-back settings, all while keeping the focus on the salary and not the person.

"Try not to make it about your peer or colleague," she said. "It's not about trying to fish around for gossip," Ms. McGurran said.

She added that the websites LinkedIn, PayScale and Salary can be good resources to find a baseline. [For even more advice on salary negotiations, see "How to Be an Ace Salary Negotiator (Even if You Hate Conflict)" in the Career Maintenance section.]

Ms. Duffy, the writer, agreed that a win-win approach is the best way to get salaries out in the open.

"When you come at it from that clear sense of, 'I'm doing this for both of our benefit, I'm not doing this to shame you,'" she said, "people are generally more willing to share."

Ms. Duffy added, "It's important to know your own worth."

# A Smarter Way to Think About Financial Decisions

BY TIM HERRERA

**FOR YEARS I HAD A 401(K) FROM MY FIRST JOB** that sat neglected, quietly collecting meager interest as I willfully ignored it. I wasn't necessarily scared or intimidated by deciding what to do with it—roll it over, change the investment allocation, leave it be; I just never wanted to address it. So I didn't.

Now, years later, I'm kicking myself thinking about how much money I left on the table by ignoring it for so long.

Sound familiar?

"There's something about financial decisions that goes beyond knowledge," Aner Sela, an associate professor of marketing at the University of Florida Warrington College of Business, whose work focuses on how people make choices, told me. "They have a unique flavor, and there's something about that flavor we don't like. They feel very cold, very abstract and analytical, and it's something that you just don't want to do."

As it turns out, there may be a reason some of us avoid making those decisions, according to a study by Mr. Sela and Jane Jeongin Park in The Journal of Consumer Research. It comes down to how we perceive ourselves.

Many tend to think that financial decisions require a similarly cold, abstract, analytical mind-set, Mr. Sela said. So if we perceive ourselves as the type of people who rely on emotion in our decision-making processes, we're more inclined to avoid making financial decisions because we think they don't "feel like me," he said.

In fact, we'll avoid making decisions about money even if we think we have the knowledge and ability to do so.

"I have a Ph.D. in business and an M.B.A. in finance, on top of a degree in architecture, so I think I can understand financial products pretty well," Mr. Sela said. "But still, every time I get a letter from my bank, my instinct is to shove it in some drawer."

The key to getting around those roadblocks is to reframe the way we think about money decisions. For example, let's say you're like me and struggling to decide what to do with an old 401(k). Rather than look at that decision as one involving stock and bond allocation and portfolio diversity, think of it in terms of the lifestyle you want for your future. Do you want to have a future in which you can eventually retire, maybe travel and have the ability to eat out a few times a week? The decision that will get you there is figuring out what to do with that 401(k).

"It's just a different framing of the same data," Mr. Sela said. "If you just call it by a different name that brings to mind different things, it certainly makes a difference."

Indeed, Mr. Sela found that people were more comfortable making a financial decision after reframing it in lifestyle terms—for example, a choice about annuities versus a choice about life experiences—even if the decision was the same in both scenarios.

So the next time you're struggling to do something about your credit report or at a loss for how to go about building your nest egg, think of it as a decision about the type of life you want to have. Future you will thank you.

## GET YOUR RETURNS

The glory days of getting an 8 percent APY—annual percentage yield, or the interest rate the bank pays you to keep your money with it—on your savings account are long gone. But with a little digging you can find savings accounts that will offer rates of 2 percent or more (compared to 0.1 percent sometimes offered by big banks).

Those returns, while not enormous, really do add up: A savings account with $5,000 in it would earn more than $500 over the course of five years.

Online banks like Ally, Marcus by Goldman Sachs, CIT Bank and Synchrony all have online savings accounts with a 2 percent or more annual percentage yield as of early 2019.

# FOUR EASY(ISH) WAYS TO SAVE A FEW EXTRA BUCKS THIS WEEK

Saving money is one of those things we all think about in the abstract but so rarely are taught actually how to do it. So, unfortunately, the onus is on us as individuals to educate ourselves about our finances.

But! That doesn't mean we all need to learn the stock market through and through, or spend days learning the ins and outs of interest rates (although those things can help). So here are a few simple tips you can do right now that can offer big returns down the road.

### 1 Up Your 401(k) Contributions

If you're lucky enough to work at a company that provides a 401(k), one of the simplest things you can do to put yourself on better financial footing is increase the amount you pay your future self. Increasing your contribution by as little as one percentage point can have truly enormous returns later in life. So go log in right now and up your contribution. That's all.

### 2 Aggressively—and Honestly— Track Your Spending

Don't do it in the "Oh, yeah, I'll look at my bank statement and see where my money went" sense. Set aside an hour tonight and obsessively pore over the last month of your purchases to see where

you can cut costs. A cursory glance isn't enough; be honest with yourself about the things you consistently regret spending money on. I use the budget-tracking app Mint, which can be as aggravating as it is helpful, but in the best way possible.

### 3 Set Up Automatic, Recurring Savings with Your Bank

Like a retirement fund, the best day-to-day saving plan is to "set it and forget it." When I examined my budget, I saw I was spending at least $25 per week on a daily cold brew. Eliminating that, of course, has not made me rich. But every Thursday, my bank now moves that $25 I'm no longer spending on coffee from my checking account to my savings account. In the nine months I've had this transfer running I've put away almost $1,000 without any effort, and using an amount that I don't miss from my weekly budget.

### 4 Stop "Saving" Money

I am the owner of a blue yoga mat I never needed, don't particularly like and haven't used once since buying it. So why do I own it? It was on sale on Amazon for $5 off, and I can never pass up a deal. In "saving" that $5, I spent $12 to buy the mat that I could have used on something I would actually use. The allure of a deal is real, and the downfall of so many of us— studies even show that thinking we'll get a deal can encourage us to spend more money than we would have otherwise. Resist it at all costs.

# Spend Money Where You Spend the Most Time

## BY ERIC RAVENSCRAFT

**WHEN YOU BUY A PHONE OR A CAR,** you do your research to make sure you get the best bang for your buck. When it comes to indulging yourself, however, you might not do the same diligence. There's one easy way to make sure that, even when you treat yourself, your money goes as far as it can: Spend money where you spend your time.

Imagine this: It's tax season and you've got a decent refund coming in. You want to use a small portion of it to pamper yourself a bit. What should you spend your money on? A nice dinner out? A new gadget? Maybe you want to spend money on an experience like some studies keep telling you to do.

Those are all good ideas, but spending money to improve the things you do every day can have the most long-term impact.

Take your bed, for example. You (hopefully) spend about eight hours there every night. Buying a new pillow or a nice bed might be more boring than a luxury cruise, but when you're still getting a good night's rest months or even years later, the benefits become clearer.

## CONSIDER YOUR "PRICE PER HOUR" WHEN BUYING NEW THINGS

However, it's not just a matter of comfort. From a financial perspective, splurging where you spend the bulk of your time saves more money than buying things that seem the most fun. For example, earlier this year, I spent $160 on an ugly, if super comfortable, office chair. I also spent $60 on a copy of Super Mario Party.

Now, a video game should be more fun than a chair, no matter how nice the chair or how dull the game. Moreover, the game cost about $100 less than the chair. So, the game must be the better indulgence, right? It's cheaper, it's entertaining and it's even an experience I can share with friends.

And yet, in the time that I've had both, I've spent far more time with the chair. I played the game about a dozen times—sometimes alone, sometimes with friends—for around one to two hours at a time. Call it 20 hours total. Since the game costs $60, that means I paid about $3 per hour of fun. That's not bad! It's cheaper than a ticket to a movie theater, anyway.

However, I've spent at least eight hours a day, five days a week in the chair (I work from home). Over a mere three months, that would add up to 480 hours in the chair. Since the chair costs $160, I've paid a paltry $0.33 per hour of sitting. After a year, that would be down to about $0.08 per hour. In order to get that same cost-effectiveness from Super Mario Party, I would have to play it for over 750 hours. The game's fun, but not that fun.

To put it simply, the more hours you spend on an activity, the more value you'll get from spending money on ways to improve it. That's not to say that temporary things are bad. Getting a massage might only take an hour and last the day, but it's still a nice treat every once in a while. You just don't get much mileage out of it.

## FIND OUT WHERE YOU SPEND THE MOST TIME

Math is all well and good in principle, but how do you make this work in practice? The first step is to find the areas of your life where you spend your time. Statistics from the U.S. Department of Labor offer some useful, if somewhat obvious, hints on where to start. According to the data, Americans spend most of their time in three key areas: work, sleep and leisure, in that order. Work takes up an average of eight and a half to nine hours per day, sleep just under eight hours, and leisure or sports activities a comparatively meager three hours per day.

Since it takes up most of your time, let's look at work. If you're in a career where you sit at a desk all day, investing in a supportive chair or a standing desk can improve your comfort. On the other hand, if you work in retail, service industries or other jobs where you're on your feet all day, then your money might be better spent on a comfortable pair of shoes.

The next biggest chunk of your time is sleep. Getting a really good mattress can be expensive, but even a comfortable pillow can help you get more restful sleep at night and wake up with less of a pain in the neck. If you're the kind of person who can't fall asleep in total silence, then a white noise machine could be worthwhile. At first glance, it might seem silly to spend $40 on a machine that does the same thing a free app can do, but over the course of a year, the machine costs less than a penny and a half per hour you use it. From that perspective, either option is cost-effective, so you can choose either one based on whatever you like best.

Then there's your leisure time. At three hours of the average person's day, it's not quite as time-consuming as work or sleep, and yet you might

The relationship between your money and your time also isn't that straightforward.

Say you spend three hours a night playing games or watching TV, but only spend an hour or two a week vacuuming your house. According to everything we've said so far, you should spend your

> ❝
>
> ### If you're going to spend money on yourself, the areas where you live your life the most are a good place to start.

spend more time on it than other, more "responsible" areas of your life like cleaning or cooking (which the Labor Department says takes up about an hour of the average person's day each). Counterintuitively, that means spending $100 on an Instant Pot for the kitchen can be less cost-effective than spending $200 on a comfy recliner.

## TIME ISN'T THE ONLY FACTOR, BUT IT'S AN IMPORTANT ONE

If being advised to buy cozy chairs instead of cooking equipment and video games instead of office chairs sounds too good to be true at best and irresponsible at worst, that's because this shouldn't be the only factor in your decision-making. You don't buy equipment for the kitchen because of the number of hours you spend cooking. You do it because it makes it easier to make food. Which, as it happens, is something you have to do. You don't need to play video games, but you do have to eat.

money on your leisurely hobbies, right? However, if you spend money on a robot vacuum, then you can reduce the amount of time that you spend vacuuming to almost zero.

That's an example of spending money to buy yourself time. You can't do much to reduce the amount of time you need to sleep, and reducing the amount of time you need to spend on work can be complicated, but buying a gadget to help out with chores or make cooking easier can give you some time back in your day. If you can save yourself some time out of your day, that might be more important than optimizing your price-per-hour number.

No single factor should decide how you spend your money, but putting your money where you spend your time can help give you some valuable perspective. You only get so many hours in the day, and you don't want to spend them in misery. If you're going to spend money on yourself, the areas where you live your life the most are a good place to start.

# What I Learned Tracking My Expenses for a Month

BY KRISTIN WONG

**AS AN EXPERIMENT, IN 2018** I vowed to track my spending for a month, the same way you might track your food intake if you're trying to change your diet.

Tracking your spending is nothing new, and money advice you've probably heard before. Maybe, like me, you've ignored this advice because you didn't see the point. I figured I already had a pretty good idea of what my spending looked like. It's not like I'm some shopaholic who can't walk past a J.Crew without whipping out a credit card, and I know enough about my expenses to know when I have enough to pay the bills and when I'm in trouble.

Nevertheless, one day I decided to look at my transaction history to see how much I'd spent in various categories over time (a feature that comes with popular budgeting tool Mint, but your bank may let you sort your transactions like this, too). In the previous three months, I'd spent a whopping $636 at Amazon alone. And what did I have to show for it? According to my purchase history, a few travel books, some shoes and a Waterpik. These purchases weren't necessarily bad, but I underestimated how much they had added up. Perhaps I didn't have as tight a grip on my spending as I thought. That's no small amount of money, and for many, it's enough to cover weeks of groceries, a car payment or even part of the month's rent.

I decided to finally heed that basic money advice and start writing down my purchases as an experiment if nothing else. It was a simple exercise, but a powerful one. And it taught me a few lessons about the way many of us spend money.

## SPENDING IS OUR FIRST SOLUTION TO A PROBLEM

Spending is often the default for most of us—the first solution to any given problem. Need to get in shape? Buy a treadmill you'll never use. Want to feel better about the way you look? Head into Bloomingdale's and buy some self-confidence in the form of a new wardrobe. There's nothing inherently wrong with spending, but it can become so second nature that we often don't even realize we're doing it, and it's especially easy when you shop online.

The simple chore of physically writing down every purchase, with pen and paper, forced me to think before buying. This short pause made me more aware of how I use money, which is often as a knee-jerk solution. For example, I wanted to learn more about Ecuador before I visited, so I found a travel guide on Amazon and hit the buy button. Problem solved. Again, there's nothing wrong with this, really, but it didn't even occur to me to perhaps borrow the book or buy it used. Spending was the easy solution.

## $20 HAD BECOME MY NEW $3

If you've never heard of "the latte factor," it's financial expert David Bach's idea that cutting back on small expenses can lead to big savings. Detractors might argue that it's slightly silly to expect that much out of a $3 cup of coffee—it's just $3, after all.

The problem with this attitude is you start saying, "It's just $3," to everything. Impulse candy at the cash wrap? Might as well buy it, it's just $3. This kind of spending adds up, but I think the bigger problem is that as you make more money, your $3 benchmark inflates. When I wanted to buy a fancy, leather-bound journal that I definitely didn't need, I found myself justifying it this way: "It's just $20, not even worth the time overthinking it. Just buy it!"

## BUDGETING ISN'T FOOLPROOF

Having written a book about money (called "Get Money"), I like to think I'm pretty good with it. And being good with money, most experts will say, starts with a budget. If you pay yourself first—save a portion of your money before you spend it—then who cares what you spend it on? Give yourself some guidelines and you can spend like the world is going out of business.

But when I paid attention to the purchases I was tempted to make, I soon realized half the things I buy are mindless, impulsive items. Sure, I budget and pay myself first, but that doesn't mean I'm spending my money in the best way possible. I could be saving more for retirement. I could be saving more for travel. When you're more conscious with your spending, you might be surprised at how much more room you can create in your budget. It almost makes budgeting unnecessary because you spend less by design and no longer need guidelines.

# HOW TO TRACK YOUR OWN SPENDING

Shannon McLay, founder of the Financial Gym, a financial planning firm in Manhattan, said she asks new clients to follow the same experiment I did: Track every expense they make, every day, for a month.

"I've had clients save over $3,000 a month just from paying attention to where they're spending their money," Ms. McLay said. "They can use apps like Expenses OK or Expense Keep, or Excel or just the notes feature on their phone."

I used an old-fashioned pen and a notebook when I tracked my spending. It was a little less convenient than an app, but it seemed to make me more connected to the exercise. I didn't just write down my purchases; I also wrote down the items I was tempted to buy, and the emotions and justifications I attached to them. This might seem a little touchy-feely, but so much of personal finance is touchy-feely. It helps to understand how you feel when you're tempted to spend, so you can watch out for those feelings later.

"After the month is up, figure out what you spent on a daily, weekly and monthly basis and determine if that felt high, low or just right," Ms. McLay suggested.

From there, challenge yourself to spend less in the following month. It's not an exercise you have to keep up with forever, but tracking is a good way to reset your spending habits and make sure you're aware of how you spend.

And that's really the goal of the exercise: awareness. It's to simply spend your hard-earned money with a little more thought. It isn't to say you'll never give into another impulsive purchase again. For that, Ms. McLay suggested giving yourself a small cushion for surprises.

"I have clients regularly save into this fund for some amount from $50 to $500 a month to cover impulses, like a surprise happy hour with friends or a pop-up ad for a dress you want," she said. "Having an account with money in it for times like this will not only control the amount you splurge but also make you feel better after doing it."

Again, budgeting isn't foolproof, but balance is important. Plan for your impulsive spending in advance to keep it tame, but track your purchases every now and then to reset your habits. You might be surprised at the things you're no longer tempted to buy when you start keeping track.

# 4

# Relate

## SELF · LOVE · FRIENDSHIP

**TENDING TO YOUR MOST** important relationships too often becomes an afterthought in a busy life. Taking a moment to tune in to your partner, your friends or, most importantly, yourself is too often overlooked. But aren't these relationships often the reason we are working so hard in the first place?

From connecting with a friend, to forging a deeper relationship with your spouse and gaining a deeper understanding of yourself, a little insight can go a long way.

Let us help you rekindle the embers on your relationships and allow you to forge stronger connections to everyone in your life.

**READ MORE TO LEARN:**

- The most significant indicators of a successful marriage

- Why you should treat yourself like your own best friend

- How to say the hardest of words: "No"

- Why you often trust the wrong people

- The importance of surrounding yourself with positivity

# Why You Should Stop Being So Hard on Yourself

BY CHARLOTTE LIEBERMAN

**"WE'RE ALL OUR OWN WORST CRITICS."** Ever heard that one before?

Yes, it's an obnoxious cliché, but it's not just self-help fluff. Evolutionary psychologists have studied our natural "negativity bias," which is that instinct in us all that makes negative experiences seem more significant than they really are.

In other words, we've evolved to give more weight to our flaws, mistakes and shortcomings than our successes.

"Self-criticism can take a toll on our minds and bodies," said Dr. Richard Davidson, founder and director of the Center for Healthy Minds at the University of Wisconsin-Madison, where he also teaches psychology and psychiatry.

"It can lead to ruminative thoughts that interfere with our productivity, and it can impact our bodies by stimulating inflammatory mechanisms that lead to chronic illness and accelerate aging," he said.

But that's not the end of the story. There are ways around our negativity bias, and it is possible to turn self-criticism into opportunities for learning and personal growth. (Really!) But first, let's talk about how we got here.

OK, so, why are we so hard on ourselves?

For one, blame evolution.

"Our brains equip us with a mechanism to monitor our mind and our behavior," Dr. Davidson said, so that when we make errors, we are able to notice the mistake. "In order to recover, we first must notice that a mistake has occurred," he said.

Just noticing that we've deviated from our expectations or goals—whether that's eating too much or not completing a daily to-do list—isn't

symptoms of depression, anxiety, substance abuse, negative self-image and, in a particularly vicious twist, decreased motivation and productivity, according to a study published in the Journal of Psychotherapy Integration. Another study, published in Personality and Social Psychology Bulletin, found that self-criticism leads people to becoming preoccupied with failure.

Basically, beating yourself up for finishing only three of the five items on your to-do list is going to

> ❝
>
> *In some cases, like when our safety or moral integrity is on the line, it's crucial that our brains tell us good from bad so that we learn the right lessons from our experiences.*

necessarily the same thing as degrading ourselves into a shame spiral. In some cases, like when our safety or moral integrity is on the line, it's crucial that our brains tell us good from bad so that we learn the right lessons from our experiences.

But sometimes, assigning negative value to our experiences and behaviors can "ensnare" us, Dr. Davidson said, into cycles of unhelpful rumination—like when you lie in bed at night needlessly replaying an awkward interaction or repeatedly revisiting that minor typo. This is where we get into the harmful, counterproductive side of self-criticism.

And it's that type of self-criticism that can have measurably destructive effects, including

make you less likely to finish those last two items—and yet we're programmed to fall into that pattern.

That seems...conflicting. What should I do?

If this feels a bit like a catch-22, that's because it is: We're evolutionarily predisposed to nitpick at our failings, yet doing so has the opposite of the intended effect.

The solution? It's called self-compassion: the practice of being kind and understanding to ourselves when confronted with a personal flaw or failure, according to Dr. Kristin Neff, associate professor of psychology at the University of Texas at Austin.

"Research shows that the number one barrier to self-compassion is fear of being complacent and losing your edge," Dr. Neff said. "And all the research shows that's not true. It's just the opposite," meaning that self-compassion can lead to greater achievement than self-criticism ever could.

In fact, several studies have shown that self-compassion supports motivation and positive change. In a 2016 study, researchers found that

"When we get caught up in self-referential thinking—the type that happens with rumination, worry, guilt or self-judgment—it activates self-referential brain networks," said the psychiatrist and neuroscientist Dr. Judson Brewer, director of research and innovation at the Mindfulness Center

> "
> Sometimes, assigning negative value to our experiences and behaviors can "ensnare" us into cycles of unhelpful rumination— like when you lie in bed at night needlessly replaying an awkward interaction or repeatedly revisiting that minor typo. This is where we get into the harmful, counterproductive side of self-criticism.

"self-compassion led to greater personal improvement, in part, through heightened acceptance," and that focusing on self-compassion "spurs positive adjustment in the face of regrets."

This is, of course, easier said than done. But core to self-compassion is to avoid getting caught up in our mistakes and obsessing about them until we degrade ourselves, and rather strive to let go of them so we can move onto the next productive action from a place of acceptance and clarity, according to experts.

and associate professor in psychiatry at the School of Medicine at Brown University.

"When we let go of that mental chatter and go easy on ourselves, these same brain regions quiet down," he said.

Developing an approach of self-compassion and a willingness to let go starts with practice. So where and how to start?

# THREE STEPS TO SELF-COMPASSION

**1** Make the choice that you'll at least try a new approach to thinking about yourself. Commit to treating yourself more kindly—call it letting go of self-judgment, going easier on yourself, practicing self-compassion or whatever resonates most.

One of the most portable and evidence-based practices for noticing our thoughts and learning to let them go is meditation. Try mindfulness meditation, which involves anchoring your attention on the breath as a tool to stay present without getting lost in judgments, stories and assumptions.

You can also interrupt the spiral of negative self-talk by focusing your energy on something external that you care about, which can help you establish perspective and a sense of meaning beyond yourself.

"If you can do things to get yourself out of your own head, like going out and volunteering or doing something nice for a family member, these things can help lift the negative voices that are going on in your head," said Emily Esfahani Smith, author of "The Power of Meaning: Crafting a Life That Matters."

**2** Meet your criticism with kindness. If your inner critic says, "You're lazy and worthless," respond with a reminder: "You're doing your best" or "We all make mistakes."

**3** Make a deliberate, conscious effort to recognize the difference between how you feel when caught up in self-criticism, and how you feel when you can let go of it.

"That's where you start to hack the reward-based learning system," Dr. Brewer said.

A part of our brains called the orbitofrontal cortex is, according to Dr. Brewer, always looking for the "BBO—the bigger, better offer."

"It compares X versus Y," he said, "and if Y is more pleasurable or less painful, it will learn to go with Y."

Think about it this way: How much better might it feel to take a breath after making a mistake, rather than berating ourselves?

"All you have to do is think of going to a friend," Dr. Neff said. "If you said, 'I'm feeling fat and lazy and I'm not succeeding at my job,' and your friend said, 'Yeah, you're a loser. Just give up now. You're disgusting,' how motivating would that be?"

This is the linchpin of being kinder to ourselves: **Practice what it feels like to treat yourself as you might treat a friend.** In order to trade in self-abuse for self-compassion, it has to be a regular habit.

So the next time you're on the verge of falling into a shame spiral, think of how you'd pull your friend back from falling in, and turn that effort inward. If it feels funny the first time, give it second, third and fourth tries.

And if you forget on the fifth, remember: Four tries is a lot better than zero.

# How to Seem More Likable

BY TIM HERRERA

**FOR MANY OF US, MEETING NEW PEOPLE** can be an anxiety-inducing affair.

Am I talking too much? Was my handshake too weak? Did I make too much eye contact? Too little? Am I boring? Are they boring, but they're boring because I'm boring?

It can be a mess! All of our worst social paranoias contained in a single interaction.

But there's an easy way to get around this, simultaneously coming off as more likable while working to build a deeper, more genuine connection with someone: **Ask questions**.

A study published last year in The Journal of Personality and Social Psychology analyzed getting-to-know-you conversations between platonic conversation partners, along with face-to-face speed-dating conversations, and found that in both settings "people who ask more questions, particularly follow-up questions, are better liked by their conversation partners." (It even led to an increase in second dates among the speed-daters.)

Those follow-up questions, the study found, are especially helpful to increase how much we are liked because they show that we are listening sincerely and trying to show we care.

Imagine that! Being a genuine, sincere conversation partner makes people like you more.

Even more good news: Although people generally tend to reflect on an initial conversation with someone as a negative experience—like ruminating on those "Did I make enough eye contact?" type of questions—it's thankfully all in our heads, according to a new study published in Psychological Science.

A team of researchers from Yale, Harvard, Cornell and the University of Essex found that after initial remarkably self-critical and negative," the authors wrote. They added that people "tend to compare themselves unfavorably with their ideal version of themselves," torturing themselves with worst-case scenarios and obsessing about how to make things better—even though there's nothing to make better because it's all in our heads.

"People can be their own greatest critic, but what is hard for people to see is that others do not

> **"People systematically underestimate how much their conversation partners like them and enjoy their company."**

interactions "people systematically underestimated how much their conversation partners liked them and enjoyed their company."

This is called the liking gap, or the difference between how much we think people like us and how much people actually like us.

The study looked at how relationships evolved between new acquaintances and found that the anxiety and self-doubt of meeting someone new can pervade any type of relationship, sometimes lasting for months.

"People are often biased by their own internal monologues, which, after social interactions, can be have this same perspective on their faults," the authors wrote.

The lesson: Remember that it's all in your head. Simply having the knowledge that any self-doubt about an interaction with a new person is unwarranted is a powerful shift in the way we approach new connections. If you feel like someone dislikes you based on a single meeting, odds are that's just not the case (and they're probably thinking the same thing).

Just keep asking those questions, listening to the answers and being as genuine as possible. Yes, it's that easy.

# Why You Should Learn to Say "No" More Often

## BY KRISTIN WONG

**HUMANS ARE SOCIAL ANIMALS** who thrive on reciprocity. It's in our nature to be socially obliging, and the word "no" feels like a confrontation that threatens a potential bond. But when we dole out an easy yes instead of a difficult no we tend to overcommit our time, energy and finances.

"The ability to communicate 'no' really reflects that you are in the driver's seat of your own life," said Vanessa M. Patrick, an associate professor of marketing at the C. T. Bauer College of Business at the University of Houston. "It gives you a sense of empowerment."

That's why learning to say no comes in handy.

One technique is the refusal strategy. A study in The Journal of Consumer Research by Ms. Patrick and Henrik Hagtvedt found that saying "I don't" as opposed to "I can't" allowed participants to extract themselves from unwanted commitments.

While "I can't" sounds like an excuse that's up for debate, "I don't" implies you've established certain rules for yourself, suggesting conviction and stability. And since it's personal, it also maintains the social connection humans crave.

Have you ever been approached by an overly friendly door-to-door magazine seller? Likely you had a nice conversation with her but ended up out $30 and receiving a magazine you never really wanted.

"We actually used the pushy salesperson scenario: selling magazine subscriptions," Ms. Patrick said. She and her colleagues asked some subjects to sell magazines and others to say no. When subjects said "I don't" versus "I can't," they were more effective in getting their point across, and the sellers were more willing to accept their refusal.

Sometimes we're afraid to say no because we fear missing out. We want to take on new opportunities and adventures, so we say yes to everything instead. It's what Shonda Rhimes and Tina Fey told us to do. But all of those yeses can lead to burnout.

"I wouldn't encourage someone who's struggling to say no to everything," said Dara Blaine, a career counselor and coach in Los Angeles.

"But I would encourage them to say no to something just to change the story, the story being, 'I have to say yes to everything or I'm not going to make it.'"

Still, some commitments and obligations are difficult to reject. You can't exactly tell your boss, "Sorry, I don't work past 5 p.m., ever." But there are ways to ease into the refusal. If your boss wants to pile on extra work, for example, you might suggest you're not the best choice for that task because your plate is already full and you don't want to sacrifice quality.

And if you're worried that your no might seem threatening, don't be. Research from Columbia University found that our perceptions of our own assertiveness are often unreliable. In mock negotiations, people who thought they were adequately assertive or even over-assertive were seen by others as under-assertive. So if you feel confrontational, there's a good chance the other party doesn't see you that way.

Each person's mileage is going to vary. But if you feel overcommitted, no is a small word that can remind you how much control you have over your destiny.

## GET COMFORTABLE WITH SAYING NO

**Practice being more aggressive when the stakes are low.** For example, when a cashier asks you to sign up for a store credit card you don't want, try saying, "I don't use store credit cards" instead of a passive "Not today, but thank you," which implies your decision is up for debate.

**Come up with a few anchor phrases for different situations.** "No, I don't buy from solicitors" for door-to-door salespeople, for example. "No, I don't go out during the week" for co-workers who want to go on a drinking binge on a Monday night. When you have these phrases ready, you don't have to waste time wavering over an excuse. And you start to develop a reflexive behavior of saying no.

**Understand your own long-term goals first.** This way, you can say yes to opportunities that most reflect your values. Second, try to build free time into your schedule so there's room for new, interesting opportunities you might otherwise overlook.

# How to Spot and Overcome Your Hidden Weaknesses

## BY TIM HERRERA

**ONE OF THE BEST STORY ARCS** from the TV show "30 Rock" is that of Jon Hamm's character, Dr. Drew Baird.

When we meet Drew, he's a successful doctor, an enthusiastic home chef and a kind-hearted animal lover who seems perfect for Tina Fey's Liz Lemon.

Alas, we eventually learn that all of Drew's success and "talents" are nonsense: He has skated through life on his incredible good looks—this is Jon Hamm, after all—and was living in "the bubble." No one ever told him that as a doctor he should know the Heimlich maneuver, or that he couldn't use Gatorade in recipes, so he assumed he was doing all of those things perfectly.

Sadly, we are all just as bad at assessing our skills and abilities, and like Drew, we don't even realize it. But there's a solution, and we'll get to that.

Research has shown that we humans are generally pretty awful at assessing our own competence and abilities, which in turn leads us to overestimate them—a phenomenon called the Dunning-Kruger effect.

The effect creates a vicious loop that boils down to this: The less skilled you are at something, the less likely you are to recognize how unskilled you truly are, and thus you

> **The less skilled you are at something, the less likely you are to recognize how unskilled you truly are.**

overestimate your abilities. Worse still, because you can't see your errors, you'll never know you need to correct them. (If this all sounds familiar, you've probably heard of the classic study in which 80 percent of surveyed drivers ranked their driving skills as "above average." Noodle on that one.)

Conversely, the better we get at something, the likelier we are to see how much more we can improve, which can sometimes lead us to *underestimate* ourselves. Similarly, those who are exceptionally skilled at something can sometimes think everyone else is at that level, making them unaware of how exceptional their abilities are. Think: impostor syndrome.

We all do this! It's simply in our nature, so it's not a behavior meant to deceive others or to unreasonably prop up our own ego. In the influential study that first examined this phenomenon in 1999, researchers found that once people realize how bad they are at something, they'll readily cop to it and want to improve.

## SIMPLE WAYS TO IMPROVE

So what can we do to stop embarrassing ourselves with, say, our awful French if we don't know how awful it is? Research suggests two routes to enlightenment.

### Ask for feedback.
It's not easy, and it can sometimes be tough to hear, but outside input is crucial to shining a light on your blind spots.

### Keep learning.
The more knowledgeable you are about something, the more you're able to identify the gaps in your own understanding of it.

# How to Have a Better Relationship

## BY TARA PARKER-POPE

**CAN YOU SPOT A GOOD RELATIONSHIP?** Of course nobody knows what really goes on between any couple, but decades of scientific research into love, sex and relationships have taught us that a number of behaviors can predict when a couple is on solid ground or headed for troubled waters. Good relationships don't happen overnight. They take commitment, compromise, forgiveness and, most of all, effort.

## LOVE AND ROMANCE

Falling in love is the easy part. The challenge for couples is how to rekindle the fires of romance from time to time and cultivate the mature, trusting love that is the hallmark of a lasting relationship.

Researchers have found that the love we feel in our most committed relationships is typically a combination of two or three different forms of love. But often, two people in the same relationship can have very different versions of how they define love. Dr. Terry Hatkoff gives the example of a man and woman having dinner. The waiter flirts with the woman, but the husband doesn't seem to notice, and talks about changing the oil in her car. The wife is upset her husband isn't jealous. The husband feels his extra work isn't appreciated.

## WHAT'S YOUR LOVE STYLE?

When you say, "I love you,"
what do you mean?

Terry Hatkoff, a California State
University sociologist, has created a love
scale that identifies six distinct types of
love found in our closest relationships:

**Romantic:**
Based on passion
and sexual attraction

**Best friends:**
Fondness and deep affection

**Logical:**
Practical feelings based on shared
values, financial goals, religion, etc.

**Playful:**
Feelings evoked by flirtation
or feeling challenged

**Possessive:**
Jealousy and obsession

**Unselfish:**
Nurturing, kindness and sacrifice

What does this have to do with love? The man and woman each define love differently. For him, love is practical and is best shown by supportive gestures like car maintenance. For her, love is possessive, and a jealous response by her husband makes her feel valued.

Understanding what makes your partner feel loved can help you navigate conflict and put romance back into your relationship. If your partner tends toward jealousy, make sure you notice when someone is flirting with him or her. If your partner is practical in love, notice the many small ways he or she shows love by taking care of everyday needs.

### Reignite Romance

Romantic love has been called a "natural addiction" because it activates the brain's reward center—notably the dopamine pathways associated with drug addiction, alcohol and gambling. But those same pathways are also associated with novelty, energy, focus, learning, motivation, ecstasy and craving. No wonder we feel so energized and motivated when we fall in love!

But we all know that romantic, passionate love fades a bit over time, and (we hope) matures into a more contented form of committed love. Even so, many couples long to rekindle the sparks of early courtship. But is it possible?

The relationship researcher Arthur Aron, a psychology professor who directs the Interpersonal Relationships Laboratory at the State University of New York at Stony Brook, has found a way. The secret? Do something new and different—and make sure you do it together. New experiences activate the brain's reward system, flooding it with dopamine and norepinephrine. These are the same brain circuits that are ignited in early romantic love. Whether you take a pottery class or go on a white-water rafting trip, activating your dopamine systems while you are together can help bring back the excitement you felt on your first date. In studies of couples, Dr. Aron has found that partners who regularly share new experiences report greater boosts in marital happiness than those who simply share pleasant but familiar experiences.

## SEX

For most couples, the more sex they have, the happier the relationship.

### How much sex are you having?

Let's start with the good news. Committed couples really do have more sex than everyone else. Don't believe it? While it's true that single people can regale you with stories of crazy sexual episodes, remember that single people also go through long dry spells. A March 2017 report found that 15 percent of men and 27 percent of women reported they hadn't had sex in the past year. And 9 percent of men and 18 percent of women say they haven't had sex in five years. The main factors associated with a sexless life are older age and not being married. So whether you're having committed or married sex once a week, once a month or just six times a year, the fact is that there's still someone out there having less sex than you. And if you're one of those people *not* having sex, this will cheer you up: Americans who are not having sex are just as happy as their sexually active counterparts.

### But who's counting?

Even though most people keep their sex lives private, we do know quite a bit about people's sex habits. The data come from a variety of sources, including the General Social Survey, which collects information on behavior in the United States, and the International Social Survey Programme, a similar study that collects international data, and additional studies from organizations that study sex, like the famous Kinsey Institute. A recent trend is that sexual frequency is declining among millennials, likely because they are less likely than earlier generations to have steady partners.

Based on that research, here's some of what we know about sex:

- The average adult has sex 54 times a year.
- The average sexual encounter lasts about 30 minutes.
- About 5 percent of people have sex at least three times a week.
- People in their 20s have sex more than 80 times per year.
- People in their 40s have sex about 60 times a year.
- Sex drops to 20 times per year by age 65.
- After the age of 25, sexual frequency declines 3.2 percent annually.
- After controlling for age and time period, those born in the 1930s had sex the most often; people born in the 1990s (millennials) had sex the least often.
- About 20 percent of people, most of them widows, have been celibate for at least a year.

## EARLY AND OFTEN

One of the best ways to make sure your sex life stays robust in a long relationship is to have a lot of sex early in the relationship. A University of Georgia study of more than 90,000 women in 19 countries in Asia, Africa and the Americas found that the longer a couple is married, the less often they have sex, but that the decline appears to be relative to how much sex they were having when they first coupled. Here's a look at frequency of married sex comparing the first year of marriage with the 10th year of marriage.

| SEX DURING FIRST YEAR OF MARRIAGE | SEX AFTER 10 YEARS OF MARRIAGE |
|---|---|
| Once a week | Occasionally |
| Twice a week | Three times a month |
| Three times a week | Twice a week |
| Four or more times a week | Two to three times a week |

Why does sex decline in marriage? It's a combination of factors—sometimes it's a health issue, the presence of children, boredom or unhappiness in the relationship. But a major factor is age. One study found sexual frequency declines 3.2 percent a year after the age of 25. The good news is that what married couples lack in quantity they make up for in quality. Data from the National Health and Social Life Survey found that married couples have more fulfilling sex than single people.

- The typical married person has sex an average of 51 times a year.
- "Very happy" couples have sex, on average, 74 times a year.
- Married people under 30 have sex about 112 times a year; single people under 30 have sex about 69 times a year.
- Married people in their 40s have sex 69 times a year; single people in their 40s have sex 50 times a year.
- Active people have more sex.
- People who drink alcohol have 20 percent more sex than teetotalers.
- On average, extra education is associated with about a week's worth less sex each year.

## The No-Sex Marriage

Why do some couples sizzle while others fizzle? Social scientists are studying no-sex marriages for clues about what can go wrong in relationships.

It's estimated that about 15 percent of married couples have not had sex with their spouse in the last six months to one year. Some sexless marriages started out with very little sex. Others in sexless marriages say childbirth or an affair led to a slowing and eventually stopping of sex. People in sexless marriages are generally less happy and more likely to have considered divorce than those who have regular sex with their spouse or committed partner.

If you have a low-sex or no-sex marriage, the most important step is to see a doctor. A low sex drive can be the result of a medical issue (low testosterone, erectile dysfunction, menopause or depression) or it can be a side effect of a medication or treatment. Some scientists speculate that

## TIPS FOR A SEXLESS MARRIAGE

Here are some of the steps therapists recommend to get a sexless marriage back in the bedroom:

Talk to each other about your desires.

Have fun together and share new experiences to remind yourself how you fell in love.

Hold hands. Touch. Hug.

Have sex even if you don't want to. Many couples discover that if they force themselves to have sex, soon it doesn't become work and they remember that they like sex. The body responds with a flood of brain chemicals and other changes that can help.

*Remember that there is no set point for the right amount of sex in a marriage. The right amount of sex is the amount that makes both partners happy.*

growing use of antidepressants like Prozac and Paxil, which can depress the sex drive, may be contributing to an increase in sexless marriages.

While some couples in sexless marriages are happy, the reality is that the more sex a couple has, the happier they are together. It's not easy to rekindle a marriage that has gone without sex for years, but it can be done. If you can't live in a sexless marriage but you want to stay married, see a doctor, see a therapist and start talking to your partner.

## A Prescription for a Better Sex Life

If your sex life has waned, it can take time and effort to get it back on track. The best solution is relatively simple, but oh-so-difficult for many couples: Start talking about sex.

**Just do it.** Have sex, even if you're not in the mood. Sex triggers hormonal and chemical responses in the body, and even if you're not in the mood, chances are you will get there quickly once you start.

**Make time for sex.** Busy partners often say they are too busy for sex, but interestingly, really busy people seem to find time to have affairs. The fact is, sex is good for your relationship. Make it a priority.

**Talk.** Ask your partner what he or she wants. Surprisingly, this seems to be the biggest challenge couples face when it comes to rebooting their sex lives.

The first two suggestions are self-explanatory, but let's take some time to explore the third step: talking to your partner about sex. Dr. Elaine Hatfield of the University of Hawaii is one of the pioneers of relationship science. When Dr. Hatfield conducted a series of interviews with men and women about their sexual desires, she discovered that men and women have much more in common than they realize, they just tend not to talk about sex with each other. Here's a simple exercise based on Dr. Hatfield's research that could have a huge impact on your sex life:

Find two pieces of paper and two pens.

Now, sit down with your partner so that each of you can write down five things you want more of during sex with your partner. The answers shouldn't be detailed sex acts (although that's fine if it's important to you). Ideally, your answers should focus on behaviors you desire—being talkative, romantic, tender, experimental or adventurous.

If you are like the couples in Dr. Hatfield's research, you may discover that you have far more in common in terms of sexual desires than you realize. Here are the answers Dr. Hatfield's couples gave.

| MEN | WOMEN |
| --- | --- |
| Be more seductive | Talk more lovingly/ complimentary |
| Initiate sex more often | Be more seductive |
| Be more experimental | Be more experimental |
| Be wilder and sexier | Give more instructions |
| Give more instructions | Be warmer and more involved |

Let's look at what couples had in common. Both partners wanted seduction, instructions and experimentation.

The main difference for men and women is where sexual desire begins. Men wanted their wives to initiate sex more often and be less inhibited in the bedroom. But for women, behavior outside the bedroom also mattered. They wanted their partner to be warmer, helpful in their lives, and they wanted love and compliments both in and out of the bedroom.

## STAYING FAITHFUL

Men and women can train themselves to protect their relationships and raise their feelings of commitment.

### Can you predict infidelity?

In any given year about 10 percent of married people—12 percent of men and 7 percent of women—say they have had sex outside their marriage. The relatively low rates of annual cheating mask the far higher rate of lifetime cheating. Among people over 60, about one in four men and one in seven women admit they have ever cheated.

A number of studies in both animals and humans suggest that there may be a genetic component to infidelity. While science has some evidence to show that there is some genetic component to cheating, we also know that genetics are not destiny. And until there is a rapid gene test to determine the infidelity risk of your partner, the debate about the genetics of infidelity isn't particularly useful to anyone.

There are some personality traits known to be associated with cheating. A report in the Archives of Sexual Behavior found that two traits predicted risk for infidelity in men. Men who are easily aroused (called "propensity for sexual excitation") and men who are overly concerned about sexual performance failure are more likely to cheat. The finding comes from a study of nearly 1,000 men and women. In the sample, 23 percent of men and 19 percent of women reported ever cheating on a partner.

For women, the main predictors of infidelity were relationship happiness (women who aren't happy in their partnership are twice as likely to cheat) and being sexually out of sync with their partner (a situation that makes women three times as likely to cheat as women who feel sexually compatible with their partners).

### Protect Your Relationship

**Avoid opportunity.** In one survey, psychologists at the University of Vermont asked 349 men and women in committed relationships about sexual fantasies. Fully 98 percent of the men and 80 percent of the women reported having imagined a sexual encounter with someone other than their partner at least once in the previous two months. The longer couples were together, the more likely both partners were to report such fantasies.

But there is a big difference between fantasizing about infidelity and actually following through. The strongest risk factor for infidelity, researchers have found, exists not inside the marriage but outside: opportunity.

For years, men have typically had the most opportunities to cheat thanks to long hours at the office, business travel and control over family finances. But today, both men and women spend late hours at the office and travel on business. And even for women who stay home, cell phones, email and instant messaging appear to be allowing them to form more intimate relationships outside of their marriages. As a result, your best chance at fidelity is to limit opportunities that might allow you to stray. Committed men and women avoid situations that could lead to bad decisions—like hotel bars and late nights with colleagues.

**Plan ahead for temptation.** Men and women can develop coping strategies to stay faithful to a partner.

A series of unusual studies led by John Lydon, a psychologist at McGill University in Montreal, looked at how people in a committed relationship react in the face of temptation. In one study, highly committed married men and women were asked

tell themselves, "He's not so great." "The more committed you are," Dr. Lydon said, "the less attractive you find other people who threaten your relationship."

Other McGill studies confirmed differences in how men and women react to such threats. In one, attractive actors or actresses were brought in to flirt with study participants in a waiting room. Later, the participants were asked questions about their relationships, particularly how they would respond to a partner's bad behavior, like being late and forgetting to call.

Men who had just been flirting were less forgiving of the hypothetical bad behavior, suggesting that the attractive actress had momentarily chipped away at their commitment. But women who had been flirting were more likely to be forgiving and

> *Men who are overly concerned about sexual performance failure are more likely to cheat...Women who aren't happy in their partnership are twice as likely to cheat.*

to rate the attractiveness of people of the opposite sex in a series of photos. Not surprisingly, they gave the highest ratings to people who would typically be viewed as attractive.

Later, they were shown similar pictures and told that the person was interested in meeting them. In that situation, participants consistently gave those pictures lower scores than they had the first time around.

When they were attracted to someone who might threaten the relationship, they seemed to instinctively

to make excuses for the man, suggesting that their earlier flirting had triggered a protective response when discussing their relationship.

"We think the men in these studies may have had commitment, but the women had the contingency plan—the attractive alternative sets off the alarm bell," Dr. Lydon said. "Women implicitly code that as a threat. Men don't."

The study also looked at whether a person can be trained to resist temptation. The team prompted male students who were in committed dating relationships to imagine running into an attractive woman on a weekend when their girlfriends were away. Some of the men were then asked to develop a contingency plan by filling in the sentence "When she approaches me, I will _____ to protect my relationship."

Because the researchers could not, for reasons of ethics, bring in a real woman to act as a temptation, they created a virtual reality game in which two out of four rooms included subliminal images of an attractive woman. Most of the men who had practiced resisting temptation stayed away from the rooms with attractive women; but among men who had not practiced resistance, two out of three gravitated toward the temptation room.

Of course, it's a lab study and doesn't really tell us what might happen in the real world with a real woman or man tempting you to stray from your relationship. But if you worry you might be vulnerable to temptation on a business trip, practice resistance by reminding yourself of the steps you will take to avoid temptation and protect your relationship.

**Picture your beloved.** We all know that sometimes the more you try to resist something—like ice cream or a cigarette—the more you crave it. Relationship researchers say the same principle can influence a person who sees a man or woman who is interested in them. The more you think about resisting the person, the more tempting he or she becomes. Rather than telling yourself "Be good. Resist," the better strategy is to start thinking about the person you love, how much they mean to you and what they add to your life. Focus on loving thoughts and the joy of your family, not sexual desire for your spouse—the goal here is to damp down the sex drive, not wake it up.

**Keep your relationship interesting.** Scientists speculate that your level of commitment may depend on how much a partner enhances your life and broadens your horizons—a concept that Dr. Aron, the Stony Brook psychology professor, calls "self-expansion."

To measure this quality, couples are asked a series of questions: How much does your partner provide a source of exciting experiences? How much has knowing your partner made you a better person? How much do you see your partner as a way to expand your own capabilities?

The Stony Brook researchers conducted experiments using activities that stimulated self-expansion. Some couples were given mundane tasks, while others took part in a silly exercise in which they were tied together and asked to crawl on mats, pushing a foam cylinder with their heads. The study was rigged so the couples failed the time limit on the first two tries, but just barely made it on the third, resulting in much celebration.

Couples were given relationship tests before and after the experiment. Those who had taken part in the challenging activity posted greater increases in love and relationship satisfaction than those who had not experienced victory together. The researchers theorize that couples who explore new places and try new things will tap into feelings of self-expansion, lifting their level of commitment.

## CONFLICT

Every couple has disagreements, but science shows that how two people argue has a big effect on both their relationships and their health.

### How to Fight

Many people try their best to avoid conflict, but relationship researchers say every conflict presents an opportunity to improve a relationship. The key is to learn to fight constructively in a way that leaves you feeling better about your partner.

Marriage researcher John Gottman has built an entire career out of studying how couples interact. He learned that even in a laboratory setting, couples are willing to air their disagreements even when scientists are watching and the cameras are rolling.

three minutes of the couple's argument could predict their risk for divorce over the next six years.

In many ways, this is great news for couples because it gives you a place to focus. The most important moments between you and your partner during a conflict are those first few minutes when the fight is just getting started. Focus on your behavior during that time, and it likely will change the dynamics of your relationship for the better.

### Why Couples Fight

A famous study of cardiovascular health conducted in Framingham, Mass., happened to ask its 4,000 participants what topics were most likely to cause conflict in their relationships. Women said issues involving children, housework and money created the most

> 66
>
> *Fights about money ultimately are not really about finances. They are about a couple's values and shared goals.*

From that research, he developed a system of coding words and gestures that has been shown to be highly predictive of a couple's chance of success or risk for divorce or breakup.

In one important study, Dr. Gottman and his colleagues observed newly married couples in the midst of an argument. He learned that the topic didn't matter, nor did the duration of the fight. What was most predictive of the couple's marital health? The researchers found that analyzing just the first

problems in their relationships. Men said their arguments with their spouse usually focused on sex, money and leisure time. Even though the lists were slightly different, the reality is that men and women really care about the same issues: money, how they spend their time away from work (housework or leisure) and balancing the demands of family life (children and sex).

**Money:** Sometimes money problems become marriage problems.

# HOW TO START A FIGHT

## IDENTIFY THE COMPLAINT, NOT THE CRITICISM

If you're upset about housework, don't start the fight by criticizing your partner with "You never help me." Focus on the complaint and what will make it better. "It's so tough when I work late on Thursdays to come home to dishes and unbathed kids. Do you think you could find a way to help more on those nights?"

## AVOID "YOU" PHRASES

Phrases like "You always" and "You never" are almost always followed by criticism and blame.

## THINK ABOUT PRONOUNS

Sentences that start with "I" or "we" help you identify problems and solutions, rather than putting blame on someone else.

## BE AWARE OF BODY LANGUAGE

No eye-rolling, which is a sign of contempt. Look at your partner when you speak. No folded arms or crossed legs, to show you are open to their feelings and input. Sit or stand at the same level as your partner; one person should not be looking down or looking up during an argument.

## LEARN TO DE-ESCALATE

When the argument starts getting heated, take it upon yourself to calm things down. Here are some phrases that are always useful in de-escalation:

"What if we…" / "I know this is hard…" / "I hear what you're saying…" / "What do you think?"

*Dr. Gottman reminds us that fighting with your partner is not a bad thing. It can help couples improve their relationships and add "real staying power," he says. You just need to make sure you get the beginning right so the discussion can be constructive instead of damaging.*

Studies show that money is consistently the most common reason for conflict in a relationship. Couples with financial problems and debt have higher levels of stress and are less happy in their relationship.

Why does money cause conflict? Fights about money ultimately are not really about finances. They are about a couple's values and shared goals. A person who overspends on restaurants, travel and fun stuff often wants to live in the moment and seek new adventures and change; a saver hoping to buy a house someday may most value stability, family and community. Money conflict can be a barometer for the health of your relationship and an indicator that the two of you are out of sync on some of your most fundamental values.

David Olson, professor emeritus at the University of Minnesota, studied 21,000 couples and identified five questions you can ask to find out if you are financially compatible with your partner.

- We agree on how to spend money.
- I don't have any concerns about how my partner handles money.
- I am satisfied with our decisions about savings.
- Major debts are not a problem.
- Making financial decisions is not difficult.

Dr. Olson found that the happiest couples were those who both agreed with at least four of the statements. He also found that couples who did not see eye to eye on three or more of the statements were more likely to score low on overall marital happiness. Debt tends to be the biggest culprit in marital conflict. It

can be an overwhelming source of worry and stress. As a result, couples who can focus on money problems and reduce their debt may discover that they have also solved most of their marital problems.

Here's some parting advice for managing your money and your relationship:

**Be honest about your spending.** It's surprisingly common for two people in a relationship to lie about how they spend their money, usually because they know it's a sore point for their partner. Researchers call it "financial infidelity," and when it's discovered, it represents a serious breach of trust in the relationship. Surveys suggest secret spending occurs in one out of three committed relationships. Shopping for clothes, spending money on a hobby and gambling are the three most cited types of secret spending that cause conflict in a relationship.

**Maintain some financial independence.** While two people in a relationship need to be honest with each other about how they spend their money, it's a good idea for both sides to agree that each person has his or her own discretionary pot of money to spend on whatever they want. Whether it's a regular manicure, clothes shopping, a great bottle of wine or a fancy new bike—the point is that just because you have different priorities as a family doesn't mean you can't occasionally feed your personal indulgences. The key is to agree on the amount of discretionary money you each have and then stay quiet when your partner buys the newest iPhone just because.

**Invest in the relationship.** When you do have money to spend, spend it on the relationship. Take a trip, go to dinner, see a show. Spending money on new and shared experiences is a good investment in your partnership.

**Children:** One of the more uncomfortable findings of relationship science is the negative effect children can have on previously happy couples. Despite the popular notion that children bring couples closer, several studies have shown that relationship satisfaction and happiness typically plummet with the arrival of the first baby.

One study from the University of Nebraska College of Nursing looked at marital happiness in 185 men and women. Scores declined starting in pregnancy, and remained lower as the children reached 5 months and 24 months. Other studies show that couples with two children score even lower than couples with one child.

While having a child clearly makes parents happy, the financial and time constraints can add stress to a relationship. After the birth of a child, couples have only about one-third the time alone together as they had when they were childless, according to researchers from Ohio State.

Here's the good news: A minority of couples with children—about 20 percent—manage to stay happy in their relationships despite the kids.

## MAKE IT LAST

Here are some suggestions for how to strengthen your relationship based on the findings of various studies.

### Stay Generous

Are you generous toward your partner? How often do you express affection? Or do small things for your

## TOP PREDICTORS OF A HAPPY MARRIAGE AMONG PARENTS

Sexual intimacy
Commitment
Generosity

So there you have it. The secret to surviving parenthood is to have lots of sex, be faithful and be generous toward your partner. In this case, generosity isn't financial—it's about the sharing, caring and kind gestures you make toward your partner every day. When you are trying to survive the chaos of raising kids, it's the little things—like bringing your partner coffee, or offering to pick up the dry cleaning or do the dishes— that can make all the difference in the health of your relationship.

partner like bring them coffee? Men and women who score the highest on the generosity scale are far more likely to report "very happy" marriages, according to research from the University of Virginia's National Marriage Project.

### Use Your Relationship for Personal Growth

Finding a partner who makes your life more interesting is an important factor in sustaining a long relationship.

Gary W. Lewandowski Jr., a professor at Monmouth University in New Jersey, developed a series of questions for couples: How much has being with your partner resulted in your learning new things? How much has knowing your partner made you a better person?

"People have a fundamental motivation to improve the self and add to who they are as a person," said Dr. Lewandowski. "If your partner is helping you become a better person, you become happier and more satisfied in the relationship."

## Be Decisive

How thoughtfully couples make decisions can have a lasting effect on the quality of their romantic relationships. Couples who are decisive before marriage—intentionally defining their relationships, living together and planning a wedding—appear to have better marriages than couples who simply let inertia carry them through major transitions.

"Making decisions and talking things through with partners is important," said Galena K. Rhoades, a relationship researcher at the University of Denver and co-author of the report. "When you make an intentional decision, you are more likely to follow through on that."

While the finding may seem obvious, the reality is that many couples avoid real decision-making. Many couples living together, for instance, did not sit down and talk about cohabitation. Often one partner had begun spending more time at the other's home, or a lease expired, forcing the couple to formalize a living arrangement.

Showing intent in some form—from planning the first date, to living together, to the wedding and beyond—can help improve the quality of a marriage overall.

"At the individual level, know who you are and what you are about, and make decisions when it counts rather than letting things slide," said Scott M. Stanley, a research professor at the University of Denver and co-author of the new study.

"Once you are a couple, do the same thing in terms of how you approach major transitions in your relationship."

## Nurture Friends and Family

Sometimes couples become so focused on the relationship that they forget to invest in their relationships with friends and family. Researchers Naomi Gerstel of the University of Massachusetts, Amherst, and Natalia Sarkisian of Boston College have found that married couples have fewer ties to relatives than the unmarried. They are less likely to visit, call or help out family members, and less likely to socialize with neighbors and friends.

The problem with this trend is that it places an unreasonable burden and strain on the marriage, said Stephanie Coontz, who teaches history and family studies at the Evergreen State College in Olympia, Washington. "We often overload marriage by asking our partner to satisfy more needs than any one individual can possibly meet," wrote Dr. Coontz. "And if our marriage falters, we have few emotional support systems to fall back on."

To strengthen a marriage, consider asking less of it, suggested Dr. Coontz. That means leaning on other family members and friends for emotional support from time to time. Support your partner's outside friendships and enjoy the respite from the demands of marriage when you're not together.

# Turning a Breakup into a Positive Experience

BY MARISSA MILLER

**BEFORE I GOT MARRIED,** anytime I got dumped I had a habit of clinging to my ex-boyfriends' oversize sweatshirts, hoping they'd materialize into the people I once loved.

As my eyes sagged like sad hammocks from under the sweatshirt's hood, my well-meaning circle of friends buzzed with advice.

"Get bangs, but don't do them yourself."

"Open an Etsy shop."

"Change your identity and move to a foreign country."

While my bone structure is in no way conducive to bangs, and I have no remarkable crocheting skills to profit from, I found comfort in being productive. Whether I was doing something radical or small, just doing something seemed more appealing than spiraling. Rather than sulking, I learned to turn my post-breakup slumps into easy excuses to better myself and do the things I never had time for. I could finally learn to enjoy my own company, either by getting to know myself better or growing into a version of myself I preferred.

Pop culture has trained us to think of breakups as excuses to binge on ice cream in the dark for a month. But that doesn't help anyone. So as you reflect on your newfound singledom, here are a few things to keep in mind.

## VALIDATE YOUR SUFFERING

Immediately booking a flight to Cancun isn't necessarily a suitable plan for everyone. Grieving takes time. It's not a sign of weakness, but rather an essential step toward accepting change.

"What I've found sticks with people seeking to be less preoccupied with something that was once very important to them is intentional grieving," said Amanda Luterman, a clinical psychotherapist specializing in sexuality.

"Consciously choose to remember why it hurts to no longer be in the relationship, and validate the suffering," she said, adding that it's helpful to think of your former relationship as a part of what makes you who you are.

Intentional grieving is a skill you can learn, just like any other.

To start, think of five memories in which you genuinely felt happy with the person. Don't discredit them. Honor your having chosen the person, force a smile and leave happy memories as positive.

"Those memories have not disappeared with your relationship status," Ms. Luterman said. "You deserve to continue to value them. You look attractive in that photo, you did go zip-lining, your costumes actually were amazing, your bravery that day was due to each other, your meals really were delicious, your laughing was real."

Playing the role of a partner or a spouse is a significant chunk of a person's identity and that's OK—but it means much of our suffering is tied to our inability to operate outside of that frame. A breakup presents an opportunity to finally learn to accept yourself on your own.

"What's common is for people to believe that if they were 'more'—a better person, more attractive, more successful, sexier, funnier or simply a more lovable human being—their partner would have loved them enough and it would have been a good relationship," said Dr. Lisa Marie Bobby, a licensed marriage and family therapist and author of "Exaholics: Breaking Your Addiction to an Ex Love."

## CHANNEL NEGATIVE ENERGY

Taking care of oneself looks different for everyone, so listen to your needs. Think of picking up a hobby without having any immediate expectations, or tackling a project you've been putting off for years without putting the pressure of completion on yourself.

"Being happy as a person on your own sets the groundwork for being the best you in other relationships, including romantic and platonic relationships," said Dr. Michele Kerulis, counseling professor at the Family Institute at Northwestern University.

"When people decide what happens in advance, it can be upsetting and anxiety provoking when it doesn't pan out," Dr. Bobby said.

Center your recovery on yourself. Bad-mouthing your ex might feel cathartic, but it's not going to help you heal in the long run. Instead, Dr. Bobby suggests alternate outlets like exercising or writing. Finding a physiological release through experiential activities helps make sense of confusing emotions like anger, grief and guilt.

If that sounds a little too abstract, it's not: Our limbic brain system that feels emotions is unable to distinguish between things we're thinking about and experiencing in reality, according to Dr. Bobby.

And then there's the "post-breakup bod," touted among celebrities as the ultimate revenge. But there's truth to exercise's healing properties.

"When stress hormones like adrenaline and cortisol are dumped into our bloodstream, our hearts pound, our muscles tense, we're sweaty and hyper-focused on the threatening thoughts we're indulging," Dr. Bobby said, adding that our feelings of anger or pain can translate to physiological pain and push us into a state of elevation akin to a fight-or-flight response.

## DEVISE A PLAN

Rein in your impulses to re-enact Taylor Swift's "Bad Blood" video—now it's time to restructure your life as a single person.

At the beginning of your breakup, document your emotions during your most vulnerable moments. Six months later, evaluate your growth, Dr. Bobby suggests. Take comfort in your control of your emotions. You have the power to steer yourself in the right direction.

"Time alone does not heal," Dr. Bobby said. "It is an active, intentional process."

Depending on your level of anxiety, you might need more near-term guidance. Ms. Luterman suggests thinking in blocks of seven days at a time so as not to do something you'll likely regret later.

"Anticipate and discuss challenging moments like running into your ex or explaining the end of the relationship to prepare and cope with difficult feelings as they arise," she said.

When confronted with the dreaded "What happened?" question at events, Dr. Kerulis suggests preparing a statement to deflect the topic. Try: "It just wasn't working out and we have gone our separate ways," or, "Yeah, we're not together anymore and I'm bummed about it. But tonight I want to focus on fun and positive things." Then transition into talking about all the fun things you've been up to in your new single lifestyle.

Still, don't fall into the trap of deluding yourself into believing that nothing tragic happened to you—it did, and it was unpleasant. So acknowledge the psychological distress and suffering that the end of a relationship can spark.

"Someone out there is walking around unsupervised with all this information about you at your recent worst," Ms. Luterman said. That's "terrifying. Your symptomatic history of being bullied, talked about behind your back, mocked and excluded is back in full swing," she said.

## TIME TO START AGAIN?

If you're no longer sobbing at the sound of your shared songs and feel the urge to go out, you might be ready to reactivate your dating app account. "Do a gut check with yourself," said Vikki S. Ziegler, family law lawyer and star of two seasons of Bravo TV's "Untying the Knot." But if those shared songs inspire you to send a 2 a.m. "u up?" text, have a trusted friend vet it first.

Should getting back together be something you're considering, Dr. Bobby recommends asking yourself these crucial questions: Are they open to making changes? Are there things you can change? Are they open to couples therapy?

She added that, particularly for couples with a long history and children, "if you're both actively working on it and if over the period of three months it feels different and gives you hope, that's a great indication it's worth another shot."

# What is the worst pickup line you've ever heard?

I was at a bar waiting for a drink in D.C. and this guy and I got into small talk. I asked what he did, and he said, "I'm a big deal." I laughed awkwardly and then he was like, "I work for the DOD." He paused, took a sip of his beer, and I said, "Oh that's neat." He responded, "Neat? Look, I know where the nukes are. You want to sleep with me, right?" I got my beer, laughed and walked away.

—**Shefali Kulkarni,** editor

When I was a bartender in the East Village, I'd go, "I live close by and there's a great deli on the way. Want to get high and eat sandwiches?" Worked. Every. Time.

—**Nina Mozes,** comedian

When I was in college and on AOL Instant Messenger a lot, a random guy emailed me. We exchanged some neutral greetings; while I thought this was someone I knew either from high school or punk shows, it rapidly became clear that he was a complete stranger. Then he asked me this: "Do you want to wrestle? Not for sport, just for fun." (We did not wrestle.)

— **Tobias Carroll,** author

A less than charming, older gentleman approached me and said, "Girl, you ain't right, but you ain't wrong, neither." You have to love the South; bless his heart.

—**Carol Walker Justice,** hospice nurse

I was once propositioned by the woman who worked in the leasing office at the building I lived in right after college. She said when I went in to pay my rent, "I divorced my last husband for someone like you." I considered moving away in the middle of the night.

— **Kevin Smokler,** author of *Brat Pack America: A Love Letter to '80s Teen Movies*

My husband actually asked me out for the first time when we were at a drag queen club with a group of mutual friends. I replied, "You know I'm a woman, right?!" He knew. I was the only lady wearing a turtleneck.

—**Karen Estes Last,** senior designer, Tennessee Aquarium

# How to Maintain Friendships

## BY ANNA GOLDFARB

**AGE AND TIME HAVE A FUNNY RELATIONSHIP:** Sure, they both move in the same direction, but the older we get, the more inverse that relationship can feel. And as work and family commitments take up a drastically outsize portion of that time, it's the treasured friendships in our life that often fade.

A recent study found that the maximum number of social connections for both men and women occurs around the age of 25. But as young adults settle into careers and prioritize romantic relationships, those social circles rapidly shrink and friendships tend to take a back seat.

The impact of that loss can be both social and physiological, as research shows that bonds of friendship are critical to maintaining both physical and emotional health. Not only do strong social ties boost the immune system and increase longevity, but they also decrease the risk of contracting certain chronic illnesses and increase the ability to deal with chronic pain, according to a 2010 report in The Journal of Health and Social Behavior.

"In terms of mortality, loneliness is a killer," said Andrea Bonior, the author of "The Friendship Fix."

We don't have to go out and spend every minute of every day with a rotating cast of friends, Dr. Bonior said. Rather, "It's about feeling like you are supported in the ways that you want to be supported," she added, and believing that the connections you do have are nourishing and strong.

An estimated 42.6 million Americans over the age of 45 suffer from chronic loneliness, which significantly raises their risk for premature death, according to a study by AARP. One researcher called the loneliness epidemic a greater health threat than obesity.

Most people aren't aware that friendships are so beneficial: "They think of it as a luxury rather than the fact that it can actually add years to their life," Dr. Bonior said.

The good news is that keeping cherished friendships afloat doesn't need to be a huge time commitment. There are several things you can do to keep a bond strong even when your to-do list is a mile long.

## NIX "I'M TOO BUSY"...

You might be booked from dusk until dawn, but without giving your friend context, that phrase "I'm too busy" can feel like a blowoff.

"When we hear somebody say, 'I'm too busy,' we don't actually know if that is true for just their lives at this time, or if that's their way of not really valuing us or wanting to spend time with us," said Shasta Nelson, the author of "Frientimacy: How to Deepen Friendships for Lifelong Health and Happiness."

"Therefore, the friendship often just dies, not from lack of anything wrong or anybody even necessarily wanting it to die, but just simply chaotic lives and a lot of distance gets put in there," she said.

### COMMUNICATING EXPECTATIONS

Miriam Kirmayer, a therapist and friendship researcher, suggests being clear about your limits when you're feeling frenzied.

"If there are certain days or weeks where you are going to be less available, giving your friend a heads-up can go a long way toward minimizing misunderstandings or conflicts where somebody feels left out or like they're being ignored," she said.

Tell your friends how long you expect to be off the radar, how to communicate with you best during this time ("I'm drowning in emails; texts are better!"), and when your schedule is expected to go back to normal.

Instead of offering vague, blanket statements about your bustling schedule, qualify your busyness: "I'm busy for the rest of the month," or "I'm tied up until the end of the year." Then make a counteroffer. If you can't meet face-to-face anytime soon, suggest a phone date, Skype session, or other way to connect so your friend doesn't feel abandoned.

## ...THEN EXAMINE YOUR BUSYNESS

If you find yourself telling longtime pals you're too snowed under to connect, it's time to look at how you truly spend your time.

"If you can find the time to binge-watch TV shows and check Facebook a million times a day," said Carlin Flora, the author of "Friendfluence: The Surprising Way Friends Make Us Who We Are," "you can make time for your friends."

Dr. Bonior agrees: "When you feel like you can't squeeze in a book club or brunch or happy hour, pedicures or whatever it is, maybe assess a little bit more. Like, 'OK, well, how am I spending my time, and might there be a window in some of that time that actually allows for a real phone call or a walk around the block at lunch with one of my co-workers that I really like or whatever it might be?'"

## PERSONAL, SMALL GESTURES ARE THE WAY TO GO

Tailored, thoughtful text messages are a low-effort way to keep up connections when you're short on time. The key is to share little bits of information about your day that your friend couldn't glean from your Instagram feed or Snapchat story.

Ms. Kirmayer suggests making messages as personal as possible to show somebody you're thinking about them.

"So remembering obviously big life events—things like birthdays are a given—but also maybe smaller things like: They had a doctor's appointment coming up or you know they were going to have a stressful day at work and kind of checking in to see how it went," she said. "Even a quick text message can go a long way."

> 66
>
> *Make messages as personal as possible to show somebody you're thinking about them.*

The author Laura Vanderkam credits tracking her time for helping her banish her "I'm too busy" mind-set. In making detailed notes on how she allotted her energy for a year, she found that "the stories I told myself about where my time went weren't always true." She suggests using an Excel spreadsheet with half-hour increments to track the day and using the Toggl app, for starters.

Once a clearer picture emerges of how one chooses to spend their time, it becomes possible to make positive, thoughtful changes.

Ask questions that invite reveals ("How was your vacation? How's your new job going?") and avoid statements ("I hope you're having a great day!" or "You're in my thoughts"), which don't tend to prompt meaningful back-and-forth exchanges.

## CULTIVATE ROUTINES

Having a regular hang with your closest confidants can take the guesswork out of scheduling quality time.

"It might sound like you're not aiming very high if you're only going to see certain friends once a year, but if you have an annual barbecue or Memorial Day party or something, where it's kind of a guarantee you'll see certain friends," Ms. Flora said, "that's actually much better than kind of leaving it up to two people haggling over schedules."

Another idea is multitask to combine your errands with some valuable BFF facetime. Ask a friend to come to your favorite spin class, join your book club or accompany you to a volunteer gig.

"The more things you can do together, potentially the more often you'll be able to see each other," Ms. Kirmayer said. "These repeated interactions are so important for keeping a friendship going."

## COME THROUGH WHEN IT COUNTS

Another way to cement longstanding friendships when things are hectic is to go out of your way to attend any milestone events—fly in for the baby shower, attend the 40th birthday party, make an appearance at the retirement party. Just show up. There aren't too many chances to make an impact in someone's life, but if you move mountains and carve out time for your friend's event, it'll sustain a friendship for a long time.

"Once in a while, do a big gesture to those friends who you really, really care about and then that will kind of power the friendship for a while, even if you're too busy to see each other," Ms. Flora said. Being that person who comes through will "make that person feel loved and taken care of even if you're not in constant contact."

## HOW TO MEASURE A FUNCTIONAL FRIENDSHIP

Ms. Nelson suggests being aware of the three areas to measure and evaluate a functional friendship:

### Positivity
Laughter, affirmation, gratitude and any acts of service.

### Consistency
Having interactions on a continual basis, which makes people feel safe and close to each other.

### Vulnerability
The revealing and the sharing of our lives.

"Any relationship that doesn't have those three things isn't a healthy friendship," Ms. Nelson said. If you're noticing a cooling with a friend, usually one of these areas needs special consideration.

Knowing what makes a friendship tick is important because it allows us to be more effective, especially when time is in short supply. "Obviously we wouldn't want a friendship to live on text messages, but it can certainly survive hectic times if we know where to put our energy," Ms. Nelson said.

## ACKNOWLEDGE EFFORTS MADE

While the energy expended to keep contact going may not always be equal, it's important to be mindful of the attempts your friends make to connect. Reach out to nip resentment in the bud.

What happens when you've done all you could to maintain a friendship but it faded anyway? There are ways to revive it:

**Ask yourself whether this is even a friendship worth resuscitating.** Like low-rise jeans and feathered hair, people can outgrow friendships, too. If your friendship was forged in a dorm room venting about homework and lousy boyfriends, the dynamic may not translate as well now that you're ferrying children to play dates and piano lessons.

**Reflect on why the friendship ended.** Was it because of a stinging betrayal; a slow process of growing apart; something else altogether? This will help you discern how receptive your friend might be to your efforts.

"The extent to which you've managed to stay in touch or how up-to-date you are on each other's lives will likely dictate how you'll go about rekindling your relationship," said Ms. Kirmayer.

**Identify what variables, if any, have changed since your falling-out.** Maybe you're in a more stable place in life and are confident you can be a better, more attentive friend this time around. Thinking about the reasons you grew apart and how things might be different now can help you take the steps needed to rebuild a closer and longer lasting friendship, Ms. Kirmayer said.

If you do want to revive the friendship, be upfront with why you're reaching out after so much time has gone by. If you miss the person, be open about that. Noting it takes bravery and some risk, she likens reconnection to initiating a courting process: "You have to show the best side of yourself, which is probably your most honest, upfront side."

If you happen to be going through a similar life experience or stage at the same time, drop a line and ask to trade stories or advice. These kinds of targeted conversations will allow for a genuine connection without coming across as intrusive or prying, Ms. Kirmayer said.

**From there, go slowly.** If you rush the integration process, you could be setting yourself up for disappointment if the friendship doesn't take hold in the way you anticipated. Be prepared for any outcome. "It takes two to start, and maintain, a friendship, but only one to end it," said Jan Yager, an adjunct assistant professor of Sociology at John Jay College of Criminal Justice and author of "When Friendship Hurts: How to Deal with Friends Who Betray, Abandon, or Wound You." "So you both have to share the goal of keeping your renewed friendship going."

It's also possible that despite your best efforts, your friend might not be willing or able to reconnect for a variety of reasons that could be personal (unresolved hurt feelings), practical (they're not available to nurture a friendship) or something else altogether, Ms. Kirmayer said.

Whatever the result, she recommends practicing self-compassion if things do not go as planned, which can help minimize sorrow and heartache.

# Three Tips to Have Better Conversations

BY JEN DOLL

**WE ALL WANT TO BE CHARMING,** witty conversationalists who can work a room and give people the comfort that they've been truly listened to.

But how?

Being someone people enjoy talking with really boils down to being genuine and being genuinely interested. But that's much easier said than done, so here are three concrete tips that will help you become a more engaged—and enjoyable—conversation partner.

## KNOW THE THREE TIERS OF CONVERSATIONS

Tier one is safe territory: sports, the weather, pop culture, local celebrities and any immediate shared experience.

Tier two is potentially controversial: religion, politics, dating and love lives. Test the waters, and back away if they're not interested.

Tier three includes the most intimate topics: family, finance, health and work life. "Some people love to talk about what they do and their kids, but don't ask a probing question until the door has been opened," said Daniel Post Senning, an etiquette expert and the great-great-grandson of Emily Post.

Note also that while "So, what do you do?" is a pretty common and acceptable question in America, in Europe it's as banal as watching paint dry. Instead, ask, "What keeps you busy?"

Debra Fine, a speaker and the author of "The Fine Art of Small Talk," has another basic rule: "Don't ask a question that could put somebody in a bad spot: 'Is your boyfriend here?' 'Did you get into that M.B.A. program?'" Instead try: "Catch me up on your life" or "What's going on with work for you?"

## BE MORE INTERESTED TO BE MORE INTERESTING

Don't enter a conversation with the intent of leaving everyone in stitches, unless perhaps you're a professional comedian.

"Channel your inner Oprah," said Morra Aarons-Mele, author of "Hiding in the Bathroom: An Introvert's Roadmap to Getting Out There (When You'd Rather Stay Home)."

"If you just talk a lot you might get exhausted, but if you ask questions and listen and draw people out, they'll think you're a great conversationalist," she said.

"For me it comes down to being aware that I should be more interested than I should be interesting," said Akash Karia, a speaker and performance coach who has written many books, including "Small Talk Hacks: The People Skills & Communication Skills You Need to Talk to Anyone & Be Instantly Likeable!"

He brought up a study in which two researchers from the psychology department at Harvard found that talking about yourself triggers the same pleasure sensation in the brain as food. "People would forgo money in order to talk about themselves," he said. You can use this to your advantage simply by listening.

## DON'T BE A CONVERSATION HOG

We've all been involved in those irritating conversations where we can never get a word in edgewise. Unfortunately, we may have been on the other side, too. Mr. Post Senning said it was crucial to "share the conversation pie. Share half if there are two of you, a quarter if there are four. The share of the pie is never as large as what involves you listening."

To be a true conversation superstar, try these tips:

- Be attentive and give eye contact.
- Make active and engaged expressions.
- Repeat back what you've heard, and follow up with questions.
- If you notice something you want to say, don't say it. Challenge it and go back to listening.
- For bonus points, wait an hour to bring up that thing you didn't say earlier.

And keep in mind that when you say something declarative, seek out the other person's opinion as well.

"If I say, 'The Jets don't stand a chance,' I'm entitled to my opinion, but I have to say, 'What do you think?' afterward," Ms. Fine said. "You don't want to be a conversational bully."

# How Your Brain Can Trick You into Trusting People

BY TIM HERRERA

**"UNCONSCIOUS BIAS" MAY SOUND LIKE** one of those ambiguously scientific terms that make our eyes glaze over and our brains tune out. But once your eyes are opened to it, you can see how it affects almost every part of your life.

Our unconscious biases are the shortcuts our brains take to reach certain conclusions. For example, when you see a completely empty subway car, your brain might assume it's empty for a reason and send you rushing to the next one. In general, these mental leaps are essential: Imagine if you had to analyze every single sensory stimulus your brain took in, then base decisions off those analyses.

There's a darker side of this process, however: Certain cultural biases can become encoded in our brains without our even knowing, leading us to draw conclusions that can be inaccurate, incomplete or sometimes harmful.

For example, research has shown that in group-work settings, instead of determining whether a given person has genuine expertise, we sometimes focus on proxies of expertise—the traits and habits we associate, and often conflate, with expertise. That means qualities such as confidence, extroversion and how much someone talks can outweigh demonstrated knowledge when analyzing whether a person is an expert.

In other words, your brain can instinctively trust people simply because they sound as if they know what they're talking about.

Khalil Smith at Strategy & Business wrote a fascinating story on the topic a few months ago, in which he cited a study that showed that "airtime"—how much someone talks—"is a stronger indicator of perceived influence than actual expertise."

take a step back when you notice that you're going along with people who only feel authoritative—either because they project confidence or dominate the conversation—and ask yourself whether they truly are trustworthy. Do they have the credentials to back up their claims? Do they talk their way around specific questions rather than address them head-on? (Khalil calls this strategy

> **"**
>
> ### Knowing that we are vulnerable to this trap is the first step toward overcoming it.

Put another way, "Whom we trust is not only a reflection of who is trustworthy, but also a reflection of who we are," researchers wrote in a 2011 study that examined how our unconscious biases affect which people we choose to trust.

As with many of our behaviors we can't see ourselves, knowing that we are vulnerable to this trap is the first step toward overcoming it. But we can also train ourselves to be more attentive to signs that we're placing trust in someone just because we perceive them to be trustworthy or knowledgeable.

Most important: Learn to catch yourself and

"if-then plans": If you catch yourself gravitating toward someone extroverted and loud, then seek another opinion.)

Two other sound strategies are to relentlessly seek outside input—oftentimes that can be as simple as asking a friend, "Is my trust misplaced here?"—and never stop learning, because the more knowledge-able you are about something, the more likely you are to know when someone's faking it.

These biases are just part of life. But being aware of them can mean you're able to find paths around them.

Trust me.

# The Power of Positive People

BY TARA PARKER-POPE

**ARE YOU SPENDING TIME** with the right people for your health and happiness?

While many of us focus primarily on diet and exercise to achieve better health, science suggests that our well-being is also influenced by the company we keep. Researchers have found that certain health behaviors appear to be contagious and that our social networks—in person and online—can influence obesity, anxiety and overall happiness. A recent report found that a person's exercise routine was strongly influenced by his or her social network.

I was reminded recently of the power of the crowd during a wellness cruise sponsored by Times Journeys. The event attracted a group of like-minded travelers who, despite experiencing various levels of adversity in their lives, including cancer, vision loss and the recent loss of a loved one, were remarkably optimistic and upbeat. The group ranged in age from 17 to 90. One inspiring man, in his 80s, had adopted a vegan lifestyle and a strict exercise routine to control his diabetes. Another new friend, a woman in her 50s who had survived lung cancer, cheered me on and kept me going during a particularly difficult workout.

After the trip, we all promised to keep in touch. Buoyed by the experience, I returned home with a renewed commitment not only to exercise and healthful living, but to simply step up my social life and spend more time hanging out with happy people.

Dan Buettner, a National Geographic fellow and author, has studied the health habits of people who live in so-called blue zones—regions of the world where people live far longer than the average. He

Mr. Buettner is working with federal and state health officials, including the former United States Surgeon General Vivek Murthy, to create moais in two dozen cities around the country. He recently spent time in Fort Worth, Tex., where several residents have formed walking moais: groups of people who meet regularly to walk and socialize.

"We're finding that in some of these cities, you can just put people together who want to change health

> **"Friends can exert a measurable and ongoing influence on your health behaviors in a way that a diet never can."**

noted that positive friendships are a common theme in the blue zones.

"Friends can exert a measurable and ongoing influence on your health behaviors in a way that a diet never can," Mr. Buettner said.

In Okinawa, Japan, a place where the average life expectancy for women is around 90, the oldest in the world, people form a kind of social network called a "moai"—a group of five friends who offer social, logistic, emotional and even financial support for a lifetime.

"It's a very powerful idea," Mr. Buettner said. "Traditionally, their parents put them into moais when they are born, and they take a lifelong journey together."

In a moai, the group benefits when things go well, such as by sharing a bountiful crop, and the group's families support one another when a child gets sick or someone dies. They also appear to influence one another's lifelong health behaviors.

behaviors and organize them around walking or a plant-based potluck," he said. "We nudge them into hanging out together for 10 weeks. We have created moais that are now several years old, and they are still exerting a healthy influence on members' lives."

The key to building a successful moai is to start with people who have similar interests, passions and values. The Blue Zone team tries to group people based on geography and work and family schedules to start. Then they ask them a series of questions to find common interests. Is your perfect vacation a cruise or a backpacking trip? Do you like rock 'n' roll or classical music? Do you subscribe to *The New York Times* or *The Wall Street Journal*?

"You stack the deck in favor of a long-term relationship," said Mr. Buettner.

One of my fellow travelers, Carol Auerbach of New York City, noted that surrounding herself with positive people has helped her cope with the loss of two husbands over the years. Ms. Auerbach was widowed at 30, when her children were just two and five. With the support of her family and friends, and her own tenacity, she was able to support her family, and she eventually remarried. And then in 1992, her second husband died unexpectedly. To cope the second time, she focused on volunteer work and contributing to her community.

Ms. Auerbach said she believes that she learned to have a positive outlook from her mother, a Holocaust survivor who left Germany at the age of 19 and never saw her parents again.

"When I was growing up we were not affluent, and the four of us lived in a one-bedroom apartment, and my parents slept on a pullout sofa," she said. "My mother never complained. I think she quietly knew that difficult things happen, but you feel very appreciative of the life you do have, and you feel a responsibility to make the most of it."

Ms. Auerbach eventually found love again and has been married to her third husband for 15 years. "Life is too short to be around negative people," she said. "I need people around me who care about me and are appreciative, and see the world as a glass half full, not half empty."

The Blue Zone team has created a quiz to help people assess the positive impact of their own social network. The quiz asks questions about your friends and the state of their health, how much they drink, eat and exercise, as well as their outlook. The goal of the quiz is not to dump your less healthy friends, but to identify the people in your life who score the highest and to spend more time with them.

"I argue that the most powerful thing you can do to add healthy years is to curate your immediate social network," said Mr. Buettner, who advises people to focus on three to five real-world friends rather than distant Facebook friends. "In general you want friends with whom you can have a meaningful conversation," he said. "You can call them on a bad day and they will care. Your group of friends are better than any drug or anti-aging supplement, and will do more for you than just about anything."

## HOW TO TURN INTO A MORE POSITIVE PERSON

### by Jane E. Brody

**Develop and bolster relationships.**
Building strong social connections enhances feelings of self-worth and is associated with better health and a longer life.

**Learn something new.** It can be a sport, a language, an instrument or a game.

**Choose to accept yourself, flaws and all.** Rather than imperfections and failures, focus on your positive attributes and achievements.

**Practice resilience.** Rather than let loss, stress, failure or trauma overwhelm you, use them as learning experiences and steppingstones to a better future.

# 5

# Thrive

## AGE · MOVE · SLEEP AND STRESS

**IT SEEMS LIKE AN OBVIOUS** choice to eat healthy foods instead of junky ones, to find time to exercise instead of binge watching another Netflix series, to surround yourself with positivity rather than stress, anxiety and negative people.

But it's not that simple. We all know we should eat better, exercise more and learn how to relax, but so few of us do it. Why?

In this chapter, we will lay out simple, low-effort strategies for incorporating healthy habits into your everyday life.

So, first read the rest of this chapter, then put the book down and, instead of just living, decide to thrive.

**BY THE END OF THIS CHAPTER, YOU'LL KNOW WHY:**

- Even one minute of exercise can make you fit

- Want to eat healthier, simply? Try limiting your sugar intake

- Strength training can build your brain along with your muscles

- Stress is inevitable, but you can turn it into a great asset as opposed to your biggest foe

# How to Age Well

BY TARA PARKER-POPE

**GETTING OLDER IS INEVITABLE** (and certainly better than the alternative). While you can't control your age, you can slow the decline of aging with smart choices along the way. Keep reading for simple ways to keep your body tuned up and your mind tuned in. And the good news is that it's never too late to get started.

## EAT SMARTER

Small changes in your eating habits can lower your risk for many of the diseases associated with aging.

**Lose just a little weight.** Small changes in body weight can have a big impact on health risks. Losing just 5 percent of your body weight has been shown to reduce your risk for diabetes and heart disease and improve metabolic function in liver, fat and muscle tissue. That means a 200-pound person can reap big health benefits just by losing 10 pounds. While we'd all love to shed all of our extra pounds, start with a 5 percent weight loss goal and keep it off.

**Avoid processed meats.** Processed meats like hot dogs and sausages have been salted, cured or smoked to enhance flavor and improve preservation. A number of studies have found associations between eating a lot of processed meats and poor health. A Harvard review found that eating one serving a day of processed meats like bacon, sausage and deli meats was associated with a 42 percent higher risk of heart disease and 19 percent increased risk of diabetes. But there was no increase in risk associated with eating unprocessed red meat. Notably,

daily cup of blueberries. But the lesson is to add darkly colored fruits and vegetables—blueberries, cherries, spinach and kale—to your diet. They are loaded with nutrients, fiber and carotenoids. They will also fill you up so you're less likely to binge on junk food.

**Skip packaged foods.** The best eating strategy for aging well is to skip processed foods and beverages. That will immediately eliminate added sugars from your diet. Think chips, granola bars, junk food,

> **66**
>
> While we'd all love to shed all of our extra pounds, start with a 5 percent weight loss goal and keep it off.

the culprit in processed meats wasn't the saturated fat or cholesterol—both whole cuts of meat and processed meats contained the same amount per serving. The big differences were the levels of sodium and chemical preservatives. Processed meats had about four times more sodium and 50 percent more nitrate preservatives than unprocessed meats.

**Eat blue (and other colors).** While you shouldn't plan your health around any one "super food," there's a lot to be said for eating blueberries. In one review of the eating habits of 187,000 male and female health workers, eating three or more servings of blueberries a week was associated with a 26 percent lower risk for diabetes. Most of us can't eat a

fast food, frozen pizza, etc. But some whole, unprocessed foods that are good for you come in packages by necessity. Think nuts, eggs, olive oil and milk, to name a few. Try to live by the one-ingredient rule. If a packaged food contains only one ingredient (ground turkey, for instance) it's probably a reasonable choice.

## MOVE MORE

A body in motion will age better than one on the couch. Consider these tips for exercise as you age.

**Exercise in intense intervals.** High-intensity interval training is less intimidating than it sounds. It just means repeating short bursts of all-out exercise with longer periods of easy recovery. In recent years, high-intensity interval training (HIIT) has generated considerable attention among exercise scientists because this type of workout seems to help people of any age and any fitness level become healthier. A number of studies have shown that our bodies get more out of interval training compared with slow-and-steady exercise. A Mayo Clinic study of 72 healthy but sedentary men and women who were randomly assigned to different exercise groups or a control group found that interval training actually led to changes in muscles at the cellular level, essentially reversing the natural decline that occurs with aging. Even if you're not an exerciser, it's not too late to start. In the study, older people's cells responded more robustly to intense exercise than the cells of the young did.

A typical high-intensity workout lasts less than 15 minutes, including a warm-up and cool-down, but has been shown in multiple studies to provide health and fitness benefits that are the same as or greater than an hour or more of continuous and relatively moderate exercise.

Want to try some really, really short workouts? Here are a few fun ones:

## The 10-Minute Workout

If you like to run, bike, row or swim—just a little bit— this workout is a great option for you.

- Warm up for 2 minutes.
- Pedal, run or swim all-out for 20 seconds.
- Pedal, run or swim slow and easy for 2 minutes.
- Pedal, run or swim all-out for 20 seconds.
- Pedal, run or swim slow and easy for 2 minutes.

- Pedal, run or swim all-out for 20 seconds.
- Cool down for 3 minutes.

Do this three times a week, for a total of 30 minutes of weekly exercise.

## The 7-Minute Workout

Twelve exercises deploying only body weight, a chair and a wall, it fulfills the latest mandates for high-intensity effort—all of it based on science.

- Jumping jacks
- Wall sit
- Push-ups
- Abdominal crunches
- Step-up onto a chair
- Squats
- Triceps dip on a chair
- Plank
- High knees, running in place
- Alternating lunges
- Push-ups with rotation
- Side plank, each side

## The 4-Minute Workout

If you don't really like doing push-ups or wall sits, you can still benefit from HIIT. Try this 4-minute burst of fitness.

- Warm up briefly.
- Run, swim or bike intensely for four minutes.
- Stop. Catch your breath.

Repeat three times a week.

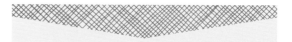
## 30-20-10 Training

This simple program will help you make the most of a short workout by improving heart health and endurance. Try it with your favorite cardiovascular activity.

- Run (or bike or swim or row) lightly for 30 seconds.
- Run moderately for 20 seconds.
- Run at top speed for 10 seconds.

Repeat the sequence five times, then rest for two minutes and repeat the sequence five times again. This routine takes 12 minutes to complete. If you are already in good shape, add another round of five repeating intervals. The next day, try a lighter exercise before trying 30-20-10 again.

**Lift weights.** Weight lifting can help you maintain muscle mass and strong bones as you age. And the good news is you don't have to lift weights like a bodybuilder to reap the benefits.

Recently scientists compared traditional weight training (heavy weights) with a lighter routine. In both, the study subjects lifted weights, either light or heavy, until the muscles were exhausted.

The scientists found that there was no difference between groups. The light weight lifters grew just as fit and strong as the heavy weight lifters. The key for both groups was to grow tired. The volunteers in both groups had to attain almost total muscular fatigue in order to increase their muscles' size and strength.

## CONNECT WITH OTHERS

Staying in touch with family and friends—and forming new relationships—can keep you healthier longer and may add years to your life.

Strengthen social ties. Make friends. Volunteer. Join a club. Stay connected. That is some of the most important advice you'll ever get about aging well. A large body of scientific research shows that social interaction—having strong, happy relationships with family, friends and community members—is an important factor in good health and longevity.

Why are close friends and family ties good for us? They give us emotional support that can help us cope with stress. They can be a positive influence, helping us create healthy habits. (If your friends don't smoke, you probably don't, either.) Studies show friendships give us higher self-esteem, and greater empathy for others, and make us more trusting and cooperative. And perhaps most important: Our friends and family give us a sense of purpose and a reason to keep getting up in the morning.

# THE 9-MINUTE STRENGTH WORKOUT

**Want a quick weight lifting workout? Here's one that lasts 9 minutes.**

The following nine moves are strength training exercises that you may have seen before. Alone, they work a set group of muscles, but strung together, these nine exercises become a complete, whole-body workout.

Dr. Jordan Metzl, a sports medicine physician at the Hospital for Special Surgery in New York, has broken down the nine exercises into three sets of three. Before you begin each set, set a timer (or work out near a watch with a second hand). If you are just starting to work out, do each exercise as hard as you can for one minute, followed by the next, until you complete the first set. Then, take a one-minute break before moving on to set two, in which the exercises should also be performed for one minute each.

| SET #1 | SET #2 | SET #3 |
|---|---|---|
| Bodyweight Squat | Forearm Plank | Burpee with Push-Up |
| Push-up | Bodyweight Split Squat | Single-Leg Toe Touches |
| Mountain Climbers | Single Leg Hip Raise | Leg Raises |
| Take 1-minute break before set #2 | Take 1-minute break before set #3 | Congrats, you're done! |

| **BEGINNER** | **INTERMEDIATE** | **ADVANCED** |
|---|---|---|
| **1 min each exercise** | **2 min each exercise** | **3 min each exercise** |
| (total 9 mins) | (total 18 mins) | (total 27 mins) |

## THINK YOURSELF YOUNGER

Aging well means taking care of both the body and the mind. Most of what we do to keep our bodies fit is also good for the brain.

**Dance like nobody's aging.** Learning while moving may be a potent way to slow the effects of aging, strengthening both the body and the mind at the same time. One study published in Frontiers in Aging Neuroscience compared the neurological effects

**Try yoga and meditation.** A weekly routine of yoga and meditation may strengthen thinking skills and help to stave off aging-related mental decline. One study compared people who took part in yoga with a group doing mental exercises as part of a brain-training program. After 12 weeks, those who had practiced yoga and meditation showed improvements in their moods and scored lower on a scale for potential depression than the brain-training group. They also did better on a test

> *Aging well means taking care of both the body and the mind. Most of what we do to keep our bodies fit is also good for the brain.*

of folk dancing with those of walking and other activities. Almost everyone in the study performed better on thinking tests whether they took part in the walking, stretching or dancing intervention. But the cognitively challenging dance appeared to have the biggest effect on the brain, suggesting that activities that involve moving and socializing have the potential to perk up an aging brain.

of visuospatial memory, a type of remembering that is important for balance, depth perception and the ability to recognize objects and navigate the world. In reviewing the brain scans, researchers found those who had practiced yoga had developed more communication between parts of the brain that control attention, suggesting a greater ability now to focus and multitask.

# Got a Minute? Let's Work Out.

BY GRETCHEN REYNOLDS

**FOR YEARS, I'VE BEEN WRITING ABOUT** the benefits of short bursts of exercise. Studies and anecdotes suggest that ten minutes, seven minutes, six minutes, or even four minutes of very hard exercise interspersed with periods of rest can lead to a robust improvement in fitness.

But I suspect that this column is the least amount of exercise I will ever write about.

According to a lovely new study, a single minute of intense exercise, embedded within an otherwise easy 10-minute workout, can improve fitness and health.

## JUST ONE MINUTE

This is good news for busy people who have tried, unsuccessfully, to fit even short workouts into their schedules. The overall time commitment for interval-training sessions is not quite as slight as many of us might wish. Consider, for instance, an interval session in which someone rides a stationary bike as hard as possible for 30 seconds, followed by four minutes or so of easy pedaling. If that person completes four of these intervals, with two or three minutes of warm-up and cool-down added at the beginning and end of the workout, the entire session lasts for almost 25 minutes, a time commitment that some people might consider unsustainable.

These concerns reached the laboratory of Martin Gibala, a professor of kinesiology at McMaster University in Ontario. He and his colleagues have conducted many of the most influential recent studies of high-intensity interval training, and many of the scientists there regularly exercise with interval training.

They, too, had noticed that interval-training sessions were not quite as truncated as some people hoped and had begun to wonder if it might be possible to lower the overall time commitment.

Then they asked the volunteers to complete a truly time-efficient interval-training program using computerized stationary bicycles. Each session consisted of three 20-second "all-out" intervals, during which riders pushed the pedals absolutely as hard as they could manage, followed by two minutes of slow, easy pedaling. The riders also warmed up for two minutes and cooled down for three, for a grand total of 10 minutes of total exercise time, with one minute of that being the intense interval training.

The volunteers completed three of these sessions per week, leading to 30 minutes of weekly exercise, for six weeks.

> **"**
> Sedentary people often cite a lack of
> time as their reason for not exercising.

But if so, they wondered, how low could someone go in terms of time and still gain health and fitness benefits?

To find out, the McMaster researchers recruited a group of 14 sedentary and overweight but otherwise healthy men and women. They focused on these volunteers because sedentary, overweight people often are on the cusp of serious health issues such as diabetes, which might be kept at bay with exercise, but sedentary people also often cite a lack of time as their reason for not exercising.

They invited the volunteers to the lab, where researchers took muscle biopsies and measured their aerobic endurance, blood pressures and blood sugar levels.

Then they returned to the lab to be retested. Their bodies were, it turned out, quite different now. The men and women had increased their endurance capacity by an average of 12 percent, a significant improvement. They also, as a group, had healthier blood pressures and higher levels within their muscles of certain biochemical substances that increase the number and activity of mitochondria. Mitochondria are the energy powerhouses of cells, so more mitochondria mean better endurance and fitness.

Interestingly, the male volunteers also had significantly improved their blood-sugar control, but the female volunteers had not. The researchers suspect that fundamental differences in how the genders burn sugar or fat to fuel exercise might affect how

each responds to some aspects of interval training. But more research is needed with both men and women before scientists will be able to understand the import of this difference, Dr. Gibala said.

In the meantime, the message from the study that most of us will grasp at is, of course, that one minute of exercise is all you need. But Dr. Gibala would like people to remember that 10 minutes of overall exercise time is involved for a total of 30 minutes per week.

He also suspects that, with this study, scientists are plumbing the lowest limits of worthwhile exercise time. "We've dropped from 30-second all-out intervals to 20-second intervals," he said, "because for many people those last 10 seconds were excruciating." Most of us, however, can complete 20-second all-out efforts without wishing to cry, he said.

Halving the intervals again, however, to 10-second efforts, probably would not provide the same benefits, Dr. Gibala said, although "maybe if you did more of them, it might work." He and his colleagues are studying these and other questions related to interval training.

For now, relying on one minute of hard exercise to ease you through the holidays with your health intact seems feasible, he said. And the exercise does not need to be cycling. Sprint up stairs in 20-second bursts, he said, or even run hard in place. The point is that time constraints shouldn't keep anyone from exercise. In the time it took to read this column, you could be done with your workout.

## THE 10-MINUTE WORKOUT

If you like to run, bike, row or swim—just a little bit—this workout is a great option for you.

1. Warm up for **2 minutes.**

2. Pedal, run or swim all-out for **20 seconds.**

3. Pedal, run or swim slow and easy for **2 minutes.**

4. Pedal, run or swim all-out for **20 seconds.**

5. Pedal, run or swim slow and easy for **2 minutes.**

6. Pedal, run or swim all-out for **20 seconds.**

7. Cool down for **3 minutes.**

Do this three times a week, for a total of 30 minutes of weekly exercise.

# Lifting Weights, Twice a Week, May Aid the Brain

BY GRETCHEN REYNOLDS

**EXERCISE IS GOOD FOR THE BRAIN.** We know that. But most studies of exercise and brain health have focused on the effects of running, walking or other aerobic activities.

Now a new experiment suggests that light resistance training may also slow the age-related shrinking of some parts of our brains.

Our brains are, of course, dynamic organs, adding and shedding neurons and connections throughout our lifetimes. They remodel and repair themselves constantly, in fact, in response to our lifestyles, including whether and how we exercise.

But they remain, like the rest of our bodies, vulnerable to the passage of time. Many neurological studies have found that, by late middle age, most of us have begun developing age-related holes or lesions in our brains' white matter, which is the material that connects and passes messages between different brain regions.

These lesions are usually asymptomatic at first; they show up on brain scans before someone notices any waning of his or her memory or thinking skills. But the lesions can widen and multiply as the years go by, shrinking our white matter and affecting our thinking. Neurological studies have found that older people with many lesions tend to have worse cognitive abilities than those whose white matter is relatively intact.

A few encouraging past studies have suggested that regular, moderate aerobic exercise such as walking may slow the progression of white matter lesions in older people.

But Teresa Liu-Ambrose, a professor of physical therapy and director of the Aging, Mobility, and Cognitive Neuroscience Laboratory at the University of British Columbia in Vancouver, wondered whether other types of exercise would likewise be beneficial for white matter.

In particular, she was interested in weight training, because weight training strengthens and builds muscles.

enrolled in a brain health study that she was leading. The women had had at least one brain scan.

For the study, which was in The Journal of the American Geriatrics Society, the scientists zeroed in on 54 of the women, whose scans showed existing white matter lesions.

The scientists tested the women's gait speed and stability, then randomly assigned them to one of three groups.

Some began a supervised, once-weekly program of light upper- and lower-body weight training. A second group undertook the same weight training routine but twice per week. And the third group,

> ## Our muscles, like our brains, tend to shrink with age, affecting how we move.

Our muscles, like our brains, tend to shrink with age, affecting how we move. Punier muscle mass generally results in slower, more unsteady walking.

More surprising, changes in gait with aging may indicate and even contribute to declines in brain health, including in our white matter, scientists think.

But if so, Dr. Liu-Ambrose thought, then weight training, which strengthens and builds muscle, might be expected to alter that process and potentially keep aging brains and bodies healthier.

To test that idea, she and her colleagues turned to a large group of generally healthy women between the ages of 65 and 75 who already were

acting as a control, started a twice-weekly regimen of stretching and balance training.

All of the women continued their assigned exercise routines for a year.

At the end of that time, their brains were scanned again and their walking ability reassessed.

The results were alternately sobering and stirring. The women in the control group, who had concentrated on balance and flexibility, showed worrying progression in the number and size of the lesions in their white matter and in the slowing of their gaits.

So did the women who had weight trained once per week.

But those who had lifted weights twice per week displayed significantly less shrinkage and tattering of their white matter than the other women. Their lesions had grown and multiplied somewhat, but not nearly as much.

They also walked more quickly and smoothly than the women in the other two groups.

These findings suggest that weight training can beneficially change the structure of the brain, but that "a minimum threshold of exercise needs to be achieved," Dr. Liu-Ambrose said.

Visiting the gym once per week is probably insufficient. But twice per week may suffice.

However, this experiment did not closely examine whether differences in the women's white matter translated into meaningful differences in their ability to think, although Dr. Liu-Ambrose and her colleagues hope to study that issue soon, as well as whether men's brains respond similarly to weight training.

They also hope to learn more about just how weight training affects white matter. It may be that strengthened muscles release substances that migrate to the brain and stimulate beneficial changes there.

Or weight training, in improving walking ability, may affect portions of the brain related to movement that in turn somehow slow the brain's loss of white matter.

Whatever the reason, exercise, including weight training, clearly "has benefit for the brain," Dr. Liu-Ambrose said. "However we are just really now gaining an appreciation for how impactful exercise can be."

## LIFT TO FAILURE

### by Anahad O'Connor

Here are two different ways to determine the amount of weight you should lift.

**1. Figure out the heaviest amount of weight you can lift one time.**
This is your so-called 1-Repetition Maximum, or "1-Rep Max." After you figure it out, use a weight that's at least 80 percent of your 1-Rep Max and aim for 8 to 12 repetitions on each set (with the exception of your initial warm-up set, which should be fairly light).

**2. Figure out your 1-Rep Max.**
Then use weights that are between 30 to 50 percent of your 1-Rep Max and aim to do up to 25 repetitions in each set.

The number of reps you do is less important than the extent to which you exhaust your muscles. You should do as many reps with proper form as it takes to reach momentary failure, which is the point where you stimulate your muscles to grow and adapt.

# How to Eat Less Sugar

BY DAVID LEONHARDT

**ADDED SUGARS, OF ONE KIND OR ANOTHER,** are almost everywhere in the modern diet. They're in sandwich bread, chicken stock, pickles, salad dressing, crackers, yogurt and cereal, as well as in the obvious foods and drinks, like soda and desserts.

The biggest problem with added sweeteners is that they make it easy to overeat. They're tasty, highly caloric, but they often don't make you feel full. Instead, they can trick you into wanting even more food. Because we're surrounded by added sweeteners—in our kitchens, in restaurants, at schools and offices—most of us will eat too much of them unless we consciously set out to do otherwise.

It's not an accident. The sugar industry has conducted an aggressive, decades-long campaign to blame the obesity epidemic on fats, not sugars. Fats, after all, seem as if they should cause obesity. Thanks partly to that campaign, sugar consumption soared in the United States even as people were trying to lose weight. But research increasingly indicates that an overabundance of simple carbohydrates, and sugar in particular, is the number-one problem in modern diets. Sugar is the driving force behind the diabetes and obesity epidemics. Fortunately, more people are realizing the harms of sugar and cutting back.

## WHAT TO CUT

Health experts recommend that you focus on reducing added sweeteners—like granulated sugar, high fructose corn syrup, honey, maple syrup, stevia and molasses. You don't need to worry so much about the sugars that are a natural part of fruit, vegetables and dairy products. Most people don't overeat naturally occurring sugars, as Marion Nestle of New York University says. The fiber, vitamins and minerals that surround them fill you up.

A typical adult should not eat more than 50 grams (or about 12 teaspoons) of added sugars per day, and closer to 25 grams is healthier. The average American would need to reduce added-sweetener consumption by about 40 percent to get down to even the 50-gram threshold. Here's how you can do it—without spending more money on food than you already do.

## FROM THE BOTTLE AND CAN

Eliminate soda from your regular diet. Just get rid of it. If you must, drink diet soda. Ideally, though, you should get rid of diet soda, too.

That may sound extreme, but sweetened beverages are by far the biggest source of added sugar in the American diet—47 percent, according to the federal government. Soda—along with sweetened sports drinks, energy drinks and iced teas—is essentially flavored, liquefied sugar that pumps calories into your body without filling you up. Among all foods and beverages, says Kelly Brownell, an obesity expert and dean of the Sanford School of Public Policy at Duke, "the science is most robust and most convincing on the link between soft drinks and negative health outcomes."

**Get this:** A single 16-ounce bottle of Coke has 52 grams of sugar. That's more added sugar than most adults should consume *in a single day.*

As for diet soda, researchers aren't yet sure whether they're damaging or harmless. Some scientists think diet soda is perfectly fine. Others, like the Yale cardiologist Dr. Harlan Krumholz, think it may be damaging. Dr. Krumholz recently announced that after years of pounding diet sodas, he was giving them up. There is reason to believe, he wrote, that the artificial sweeteners they contain lead to "weight gain and metabolic abnormalities."

## THE SODA ALTERNATIVE

Many people who think they're addicted to soda are attracted to either the caffeine or the carbonation in the drink. You can get caffeine from coffee and tea (lightly sweetened or unsweetened), and you can get carbonation from seltzer, flavored or otherwise.

For many people, the shift to seltzer, club soda or sparkling water is life changing. It turns hydration into a small treat that's still calorie-free. Buy yourself a seltzer maker, as I have, and gorge on the stuff at home, while saving money. Or buy fizzy water in cans or bottles. Sales of carbonated water have more than doubled since 2010, with the brand La Croix now offering more than 20 different flavors, all without added sugar.

If they're not sweet enough for you, you can also add a dash of juice to plain seltzer. But many people find that they lose their taste for soda after giving it up. And many Americans are giving it up: Since the late 1990s, sales of full-calorie soda have fallen more than 25 percent.

# FIRST THING IN THE MORNING

Breakfast is the most dangerous meal of the day for sugar. Many breakfast foods that sound as if they're healthy are, in fact, laden with sugar. In Chobani Strawberry Yogurt, for example, the second ingredient—ahead of strawberries!—is evaporated cane sugar. And many brands of granola have more sugar per serving than Froot Loops or Cocoa Puffs. In the United States, as the science writer Gary Taubes says, breakfasts have become "lower-fat versions of dessert."

There are two main strategies to ensure that breakfast doesn't become a morning dessert. The first is for people who can't imagine moving away from a grain-based breakfast, like cereal or toast. If you fall into this category, you have to be quite careful, because processed grains are often packed with sugar.

A few grain-based breakfasts with no or very low sugar:

- **Cheerios.** They're quite low in sugar.
- **Plain oatmeal.** Flavor it with fresh fruit and, if necessary, a small sprinkling of brown sugar.
- **Bread.** A few breads have no sugar (like Ezekiel 4:9 Whole Grain). A longer list have only one gram, or less, per slice (including Sara Lee Whole Wheat and Nature's Own Whole Wheat). Authentic Middle Eastern breads, like pita and lavash, are particularly good options, and a growing number of supermarkets sell them. Avoid the overly processed pita-style breads.
- **Homemade granola.** You can also make your own granola and play around with the sugar amounts.

But there is also a more creative alternative. Move away from grain-based breakfasts. If you do that, avoiding added sugar is easy. Try one of the following:

- **Scrambled or fried eggs**
- **Fruit**
- **Plain yogurt**
- **A small piece of toast**
- **A few nuts**
- **A small portion of well-spiced vegetables, like spinach, carrots and sweet potatoes.**

**A final tip:** Keep your juice portions small. Real juice doesn't have added sweeteners. But fruit juice is one source of natural sugars that can be dangerous, because of how efficiently it delivers those sugars. Keep your juice portions to no more than six ounces, and have only one per day.

## THE SAUCE RISK

Other than breakfast, sauces and toppings are the biggest stealth sugar risk.

Two of the four biggest ingredients in Heinz Ketchup are sweeteners. The biggest ingredient in many barbecue sauces is high fructose corn syrup. Many pickles—especially those labeled "bread and butter"—are heavily sweetened. Not only does Ragu pasta sauce have added sugar but so does Newman's Own Marinara. Even Grey Poupon Dijon Mustard has some added sugar.

It is easy enough to use sauces without sugar in most cases. These products are good examples of sauces that forgo the sugar:

- Maille dijon mustard
- Gulden's spicy brown mustard
- French's yellow mustard
- Prego's marinara sauce
- Victoria pasta sauces
- Vlasic Kosher Dill Pickles
- Newman's Own Classic Oil and Vinegar salad dressing

## MAKE YOUR OWN

Want to control what's in your sauces? Make them yourself. You can quickly and cheaply make your own salad dressing with some combination of olive oil, an acid (like vinegar, lemon or lime), herbs, garlic and shallots.

## DON'T RUIN IT ALL AT THE END OF A MEAL

Eating dessert is one of the great little joys of life, and we're not going to tell you that you can't have dessert. Have dessert! Just keep three items in mind:

**Portion size.** Many standard American desserts have become grotesquely large. Instead, think of two or three Oreos, or a different dessert of similar size, as a normal dessert. Anything larger is a big splurge, the sort of indulgence to reserve for special occasions.

**Habits.** If you want to keep your sugar consumption under control, you can help yourself by getting out of the habit of having a full artificially sweetened dessert every night. There are other end-of-day rituals that can help you fill the void, like a cup of tea or...

**Fruit.** Fruit is really a miracle food. It's sweet, delicious and full of nutrients and fiber. Yes, it's possible to eat so much fruit that you end up getting too much sugar in your diet. But very few people have this problem. For people who want a sweet every day, fruit is the way to go.

Some tips on picking great fruits:

- Eat it fresh.
- Experiment with new fruits (like pomelos and papaya).
- Eat it dried (Trader Joe's excels here).
- Eat it jarred or canned in the winter. (Just avoid all the fruit that comes with extra sweeteners.)

The beauty of fruit helps to underscore the overriding point about sugar. It's normal to have some sugar in your diet. The problem is all of the processed sugar that has snuck into the modern diet. It's so prevalent that you need a strategy for avoiding it. Once you come up with a strategy, eating a healthy amount of sugar isn't nearly as hard as it sometimes seems.

## CHECK YOUR PANTRY

Food makers sneak sugar into more foods than you may realize. It's in many brands of chicken stock, soup, salami, smoked salmon, tortillas and crackers. And most of these foods do not need sweeteners to taste good.

If you take a little time to look at labels—at the grocery store or online— you can quickly learn which staples have sugar and which don't. Here's a sampling of some quick switches you could make:

| FOOD | ADDED SUGAR | NO SUGAR |
|---|---|---|
| Crackers | Wheat Thins, Ritz | Triscuits, Saltines |
| Flour Tortillas | Mission | Guerrero |
| Chicken Broth | Swanson | College Inn, Pacific |

### TRY IT:

When you go to the supermarket, compare various brands, and choose one with little added sugar. Do this once, and then it's easy to make the no-sugar items your default. You no longer have to spend energy thinking about it.

## What is your worst health habit?

Even though I'm always telling people to drop things from their to-do lists, I'm constantly over-committing myself. Throughout the fall, I felt behind, and I finally caught up going into Thanksgiving week. I had an empty to-do list; I didn't work much over the holidays. Feeling like I had a ton of flexibility, I proactively offered to read and give feedback on three different people's book drafts. Within two days, I was like, what the hell was I thinking? I would have never advised anyone in my position to do this, but I am my own worst enemy. The upside is that they were all really excellent books.

— **Adam Grant, Ph.D.,** host of the "WorkLife" podcast and *New York Times* best-selling author of *Give and Take*, *Originals*, and *Option B*

People might say I should feel guilty about this, but I don't feel guilty: I drink a lot of diet soda. I drink as much as I want, and I don't worry about it. I love Diet Coke, the terrific new Diet Coke flavors, Coke Zero, Diet Cherry Coke, Fresca, Diet Dr Pepper, and all the rest. I'm a low-carb eater, so I don't eat sugar, flour, rice or starchy vegetables. We have a limited amount of energy to direct toward making better habits.

— **Gretchen Rubin,** author of *Outer Order, Inner Calm* (March 2019), as well as the *New York Times* bestsellers *The Four Tendencies*, *Better Than Before*, and *The Happiness Project*

As soon as I have an injury, I start to think like my patients tend to do: This is going to go away. I'll give it a few weeks. I'll modify my activity. When the injury doesn't get better, I think: You need to go to the next step. But where am I going to find the time? My life is way too busy. I can't do it. I will start some kind of rehab on my own, but it's not the same as physical therapy, and what I should be doing four or five days a week, I'm doing once a week, and dedicating a whole 5 or 10 minutes instead of 45. It just takes a lot to finally say enough is enough and do it properly and see someone.

— **Dr. Dennis Cardone,** chief of primary care sports medicine at NYU Langone Health

# How to Be Better at Sleep

BY TARA PARKER-POPE

**MOST PEOPLE KNOW THEY NEED** to eat right and exercise to be healthy. But what about sleep? We spend about a third of our lives asleep, and sleep is essential to better health. But many of us are struggling with sleep. Four out of five people say that they suffer from sleep problems at least once a week and wake up feeling exhausted. So how do you become a more successful sleeper? Grab a pillow, curl up and keep reading to find out.

## HOW MUCH SLEEP DO YOU REALLY NEED?

If you wake up tired, chances are you're not getting enough sleep.

### The Magic Number

The best person to determine how much sleep you need is you. If you feel tired, you probably need more sleep. But science does offer some more specific guidance. People who sleep seven hours a night are healthier and live longer. Sleeping less than seven hours is associated with a range of health problems, including obesity, heart disease, depression and impaired immune function. But sleep needs vary greatly by individual. Age, genetics, lifestyle and environment all play a role. Follow these steps to determine if you're getting enough sleep for your body and lifestyle.

## Ask: Are You Sleepy?

That simple question is the best way to determine if you're getting adequate sleep. If you often feel tired at work, long for a nap or fall asleep on your morning or evening commute, your body is telling you that it's not getting enough sleep. If you're getting seven or eight hours of sleep a night but are still feeling tired and sleep-deprived, you may be suffering from interrupted sleep or a sleep disorder and may need to talk to a doctor and undergo a sleep study.

Do you find yourself making friends with the snooze button after staying up all night? There are things you can do to change that.

## BECOME A MORNING PERSON

Like most creatures on earth, humans come equipped with a circadian clock, a roughly 24-hour internal timer that keeps our sleep patterns in sync with our planet. At least until genetics, age and our personal habits get in the way. Even though the average adult needs eight hours of sleep per night, there are "shortsleepers," who need far less, and morning people, who, research shows, often come from families of other morning people. Then there are the rest of us, who rely on alarm clocks.

For those who fantasize about greeting the dawn, there is hope. With a little focus, discipline and patience, you have the ability to reset your own internal clock. But be warned, it's not easy. Changing

## 5 STEPS TO BECOMING A MORNING PERSON

**STEP 1**
Set a wake-up goal.

**STEP 2**
Move your current wake-up time by 20 minutes a day. If you regularly rise at 8 a.m., but really want to get moving at 6 a.m., set the alarm for 7:40 on Monday. The next day, set it for 7:20, and so on.

**STEP 3**
Avoid extra light exposure from computers or televisions as you near bedtime. Go to bed when you are tired.

**STEP 4**
When your alarm goes off in the morning, don't linger in bed. Hit yourself with light.

**STEP 5**
Go to bed a little earlier the next night. In theory, you'll gradually get sleepy about 20 minutes earlier each night.

*A word of warning: Note that while this method works for many, it doesn't work for everyone. Very early risers and longtime night owls have a hard time ever changing.*

# KEEP A SLEEP DIARY

Even if you think you're getting enough sleep, you may be surprised once you see your sleep patterns in black and white. Some of the new activity trackers will monitor your sleep patterns for you, but you can also do it easily yourself. For the next week, keep a sleep diary. Write down the time you go to bed and the hour you wake up. Write down your total hours of sleep and whether you took naps or woke up in the middle of the night. Note how you felt in the morning. Refreshed and ready to conquer the world? Or groggy and fatigued? Not only will a sleep diary give you insights into your sleep habits, but it will be useful to your doctor if you think you are suffering from a sleep disorder.

## SAMPLE SLEEP CHART

| NIGHT | BEDTIME | DAY | WAKE-UP TIME | TOTAL HOURS | SLEEP NOTES (wake-ups, time to fall asleep, daytime sleepiness, etc.) |
|---|---|---|---|---|---|
| Sun | | Mon | | | |
| Mon | | Tue | | | |
| Tue | | Wed | | | |
| Wed | | Thu | | | |
| Thu | | Fri | | | |
| Fri | | Sat | | | |
| Sat | | Sun | | | |

your sleep pattern requires commitment, and it means changing old habits. No more TV-watching marathons late into the night.

Changing your internal sleep clock requires inducing a sort of jet lag without leaving your time zone. And sticking it out until your body clock resets itself. And then not resetting it again. Here's how to become more of a morning person.

## HOW TO WAKE UP

If you are struggling to wake up in the morning, sleep experts suggest a few simple ways to train your body.

**Buy a louder alarm.** It may sound silly, but if you regularly sleep through your alarm, you may need a different alarm. If you use your phone alarm, change up the ring tone and set the volume on high.

**Sunlight.** One of the most powerful cues to wake up the brain is sunlight. Leaving your blinds open so the sun shines in will help you wake up sooner if you regularly sleep late into the day.

**Eat breakfast.** Eating breakfast every day will train your body to expect it and get you in sync with the morning. If you've ever flown across time zones, you'll notice that airlines often serve scrambled eggs and other breakfast foods to help passengers adjust to the new time zone.

**Don't blow it on the weekend.** Besides computer screens, the biggest saboteur for an aspiring morning person is the weekend. Staying up later on Friday or sleeping in on Saturday sends the brain an entirely new set of scheduling priorities. By Monday, a 6 a.m. alarm will feel like 4 a.m. Stick to your good sleep habits, even on the weekends.

## NEED MOTIVATION?

Tired people are not happy, healthy or safe. Here are some of the things that go wrong when you don't get enough sleep.

**Sleep and illness.** People who get less than seven hours of sleep a night are more likely to have chronic health problems like obesity, heart disease, diabetes, high blood pressure, stroke, depression and premature death. While the long-term health risks of bad sleep are enough to keep you awake at night, there's more bad news. You're also more likely to catch a cold. In one surprising study, researchers found 164 men and women who were willing to take nose drops that exposed them to the cold virus. (That's not the most surprising part of the story.) You might think that everyone who willingly puts a cold virus in their nose would get sick, but they don't. A healthy immune system can fight off a cold. But not a sleep-deprived immune system. The people most likely to get sick from the cold-infused nose drops? Those who got six or fewer hours of sleep.

**The tired brain.** A tired brain is not a wise brain, and people who are sleep deprived make more mistakes. The American Insomnia Survey published in 2012 estimated that 274,000 workplace accidents were directly related to sleep problems. The bill for these sleep-deprived mistakes? $31 billion annually.

Why does this happen? While the body goes into rest mode during sleep, the brain becomes highly

> **Drowsy driving is as much of a safety risk as drunk driving or texting and driving.**

active. Think of it like a computer or a smartphone. You use the nighttime to back up all your data, and so does your brain. One of its big jobs is to consolidate memories, link with old memories and create paths for you to retrieve memories. It also forms connections between disparate thoughts and ideas. That's why sometimes, when you wake up, a big idea suddenly pops into your head. And it's why, when you don't sleep, your thinking and memory are fuzzy. Some research suggests that when you don't sleep (like when students pull an all-nighter), your ability to learn new information drops by almost half.

**Driving while tired.** Drowsy driving is as much of a safety risk as drunk driving or texting and driving. Studies show that going without sleep for 20 to 21 hours and then getting behind the wheel is comparable to having a blood alcohol level of about .08 percent, which is the legal limit in most states. If you're awake for 24 hours, that's the blood alcohol equivalent of 0.1 percent, which is higher than the legal limit in all the states.

You are at risk for drowsy driving if you get less than six hours of sleep at night. Snorers also are at risk, because snoring is a sign of sleep apnea and interrupted sleep.

In 2009, an estimated 730 deadly motor vehicle accidents involved a driver who was either sleepy or dozing off, and an additional 30,000 crashes that were nonfatal involved a drowsy driver. Accidents involving sleepy drivers are more likely to be deadly or cause injuries, in part because people who fall asleep at the wheel either fail to hit their brakes or veer off the road before crashing.

Groggy drivers often blast the radio or roll down the window to stay awake, but those measures don't really work, say experts. Coffee or caffeinated drinks may help, but some individuals don't get much of an effect. The best advice if you find yourself sleepy at the wheel: Pull over for a quick catnap.

**Sleep and weight gain.** For years researchers have known that adults who sleep less than five or six hours a night are at higher risk of being overweight. Among children, sleeping less than 10 hours a night is associated with weight gain. Some research even shows that losing just a few hours of sleep a few nights in a row can lead to almost immediate weight gain.

Part of the reason may be that sleep-deprived people eat more. Staying up late and skimping on sleep leads to more eating in general, and a hankering for carbohydrates. In one study, sleep-deprived eaters ended up eating more calories during after-dinner snacking than in any other meal during the day. By the end of the first week the sleep-deprived subjects had gained an average of about two pounds. Overall, people consumed 6 percent more calories when they got too little sleep. Once they started sleeping more, they began eating more healthfully, consuming fewer carbohydrates and fats.

## SLEEP HABITS

The first step toward better sleep is to develop better "sleep hygiene"—those daily habits that allow you to train your body for sleep.

**Bedtime:** Go to bed at about the same time every night, including weekends.

**Don't sleep in:** Keep your wake-up time consistent. Don't sleep in on the weekends.

**Naps:** If you take a nap, set the alarm so you don't sleep for more than an hour. Don't take a nap after 3 p.m.

**Keep to a schedule:** Schedules aren't just about bedtime and wake-up time. It also means eating your meals, taking medications, exercising and even watching television should occur about the same time every day to keep your body clock in sync.

**Avoid screens:** Turn off the tablet, the television and the phone. The blue light in your screen has the same effect on your brain as sunlight, which means it wakes you up just when you want to be drifting off.

**Think spa bedroom:** Make your bedroom a pleasant, peaceful and relaxing getaway. Get rid of exercise equipment, televisions, small children, etc.

## KEEP IT COOL

Cool bodies sleep better, but most people keep their bedrooms too warm at night, which can interfere with sleep. Taking a hot bath before bedtime is a good idea, because once you get out of the bath, your body cools down more quickly, which will help you drift off to sleep.

**Beds are for sleep and romance:** Don't use the bed for watching television, talking on the phone, doing homework or eating and drinking.

**Work out early:** Strenuous exercise is not a good idea right before bedtime. Try yoga.

**No night eating:** Don't eat meals close to bedtime and avoid evening and late-night snacking. If your body is churning through a big meal, it's certainly not going to get the rest it needs. And if you're overweight or prone to digestion problems, you're likely to experience painful heartburn and reflux if you binge too close to bedtime.

**Catch some morning rays:** Sunlight keeps your internal clock ticking. Go outside as soon as you wake up and spend at least 15 minutes in the morning sun. (And use sunscreen.)

# How to Be Better at Stress

BY TARA PARKER-POPE

**STRESS IS UNAVOIDABLE IN MODERN LIFE,** but it doesn't have to get you down. Work, money and family all create daily stress, while bigger issues like politics and terrorism contribute to our underlying stress levels. But approach it the right way, and it won't rule your life; it can even be good for you.

## TAKE CONTROL

Stress is inevitable; getting sick from it is not.

### The Perception of Stress

While we know that stress is associated with health problems, plenty of people with high-stress lives are thriving. How is that possible? In 2012, researchers from the University of Wisconsin–Madison published a seminal study looking at how 28,000 people perceived stress in their lives. People in the study answered these two questions:

contracting a virus a second time, regular exposure to small amounts of stress can inoculate you from the most detrimental effects of stress when you suffer a big stressful event in your life.

## STILL SKEPTICAL?

Think about how firefighters train. They educate themselves about fire and how it behaves in different situations. They put themselves through grueling physical training to practice carrying heavy equipment, navigating dark, smoky buildings and stairwells, and braving the heat of a raging fire. They practice running into burning buildings. The training is hard and highly stressful.

Now imagine you are out for a nightly walk and you see that a neighbor's house is on fire. Your heart races. You panic. You fumble with your phone. You take a step toward the house. You hesitate. What do you do? Fortunately, the firefighters arrive and race into the home without hesitation. Your moment of stress and anxiety is just another day at the office for them. They know what to expect. They trained for it.

You can practice for everyday stress in similar ways, by putting yourself in challenging situations. The good news is that practicing stress can actually be enjoyable, even thrilling. The key is to push yourself out of your comfort zone. Here are some suggestions:

- Run a marathon.
- Play in a Scrabble competition.
- Read an original poem at a poetry slam.
- Climb a mountain.
- Tell a story in front of a crowd.

- Take on a tough project at work.
- Kayak the Colorado rapids.
- Attend a boot camp.

Not only will challenging experiences give you more confidence, but the repeated exposure to stressful situations will also change your body's biological response to stress. Your stress hormones become less responsive, allowing you to better handle stress when it comes.

## AN RX FOR RESILIENCE

Another factor in how you handle a stressful situation is resilience. The American Psychological Association defines resilience this way:

> **Resilience** is the process of adapting well in the face of adversity, trauma, tragedy, threats or significant sources of stress—such as family and relationship problems, serious health problems or workplace and financial stressors. It means "bouncing back" from difficult experiences.

You can boost your resilience in a number of ways. In the book "Resilience: The Science of Mastering Life's Greatest Challenges," the authors, Dr. Steven M. Southwick and Dr. Dennis S. Charney, studied people who experienced great stressors—prisoners of war, men in the special forces, victims of trauma or survivors of catastrophic events. They found that people with the most resilience in the face of extreme challenges shared several behaviors and mind-sets. From that research, the duo identified 10 factors associated with resilience. You don't need to practice all 10 behaviors to build resilience; just pick the two or three or four that speak to you.

- **Adopt a positive attitude.** Optimism is strongly related to resilience.
- **Reframe the situation.** Just as the stressed-out study subjects were taught to reappraise stress as their friend, people who are resilient typically reframe a negative situation as an opportunity for growth, learning or change.
- **Focus on core beliefs.** People with a deeply held core belief, strong faith or a commitment to altruism often show more resilience.
- **Find a role model.** Seeing someone else who has come through adversity can strengthen your own resilience.
- **Face your fears.** Confronting a challenge rather than avoiding it will help you cope and build confidence.
- **Fall back on religion or spirituality.** For many people, strong faith or spiritual beliefs can fuel resilience.
- **Seek social support.** People who reach out to friends, family and support groups fare better during stressful times.
- **Exercise.** It improves mood, relieves stress and makes you physically stronger.
- **Inoculate against stress.** Challenge yourself regularly in the areas of emotional intelligence, moral integrity and physical endurance.
- **Find meaning and purpose.** Having a clear purpose in life can boost your emotional strength during difficult times.

## EXERCISE

Numerous studies have shown that exercise can improve your mood.

Exercise can channel your stress response into something constructive and distract your mind from the challenges at work or home that make you feel chronically stressed. In many ways exercise appears to be a form of stress inoculation. In studies, mice given access to running wheels and tubes to explore for just two weeks became resistant to stress compared with mice that had not exercised. They measured this by exposing the mice to an aggressive mouse. After the bullying, the exercising mice bounced back, but the sedentary mice continued to show signs of stress. The bottom line: Exercise doesn't eliminate stress, but it does give your body the physical conditioning it needs to recover from it.

### How much exercise do I need to manage stress?

It doesn't take much. Even small amounts of exercise can help you manage your stress. The key is consistency. Don't let the stress of your day push exercise off the schedule.

### Does the type of exercise matter?

The exercise that is best for relieving stress is the one you will do consistently. Find something that fits your schedule and that you enjoy. For some, that will be a morning spin class or an evening run. For others, it will be a 30-minute walk at lunchtime. A Norwegian study found that people who engaged in any exercise, even a small amount, reported improved mental health compared with people who never exercised.

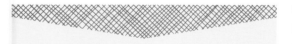

## TAKE IT OUTSIDE

Simply taking your exercise outdoors can have a significant effect on your mood.

In a number of recent studies, volunteers who walked outdoors reported enjoying the activity more than those who walked indoors on a treadmill. Subsequent psychological tests showed outdoor exercisers scored significantly higher on measures of vitality, enthusiasm, pleasure and self-esteem and lower on tension, depression and fatigue.

A few small studies have found that people have lower blood levels of cortisol, a hormone related to stress, after exerting themselves outside as compared with inside. There's speculation, too, that exposure to direct sunlight, known to affect mood, plays a role.

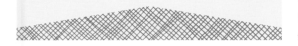

## What about weight training?

One study showed that six weeks of bicycle riding or weight training eased symptoms in women who received a diagnosis of anxiety disorder. The weight training was especially effective at reducing irritability.

Indeed, some research suggests that when it comes to reducing stress, you'll get more out of exercise if you incorporate some weight training.

Studies show that anaerobic or resistance exercises (working with weights) taxes muscles more than aerobic exercise like walking or running. The result is that weight training, done right, may produce more mood-boosting endorphins than cardio exercise. Exercises that stress the large muscles seem to have the biggest effect, like squats, leg presses, incline sit-ups, military presses and bench presses.

Don't go for a powerlifting record. The best weight training to manage stress consists of three moderate-weight sets of 10 repetitions with one minute of rest. The U.S. Army Research Institute of Environmental Medicine found that this 3-10-1 moderate weight strategy produced more endorphins than using heavier weights for five reps and a three-minute rest.

## MIND

Exercise your mind and let it rest to help it better process stress.

### Giving Your Mind a Rest

For people dealing with high levels of stress, it can be hard to fathom how a few moments of meditation will help. After meditation, the stressors are still there—you're still getting divorced, caring for an aging parent, struggling with the demands of a high-stress job. How can a few moments of deep thought possibly help your life?

It may help to think about how muscles get stronger. Unrelenting exercise simply tears down a muscle and leads to injury. Smart exercisers know the value of a day of rest—that's when your muscles regenerate and come back stronger than before.

# WRITE IT DOWN

Another way to cope with stress: writing. Here are some ideas to get you started.

## JOURNAL EVERY DAY.

Just writing about your thoughts, feelings and experiences every day can help. Explore your thoughts and feelings about an issue. Don't just relive the stress in your life, but try to find meaning in it or explore how well you've handled certain situations. Be disciplined and write at the same time every day so it becomes a habit. In a University of Texas study, students who wrote about stressful or traumatic events for four days in a row reaped the benefits for months after. For the next six months, the writing students had fewer visits to the campus health center and used fewer pain relievers than the students in the experiment who wrote about trivial matters.

## CHANGE YOUR STORY.

Use writing to force yourself to confront the changes you need to make in your life. On the first day, write down your goals, then write down why you haven't achieved them. ("I don't have the time or the money," "Too many family responsibilities," etc.) The next day review your writing. Now ask: What is really standing in the way of your goals? Change the story so you have control. Maybe the answer is: I don't put myself first. I don't make exercise a priority. I let other people talk me into spending money rather than saving.

## WRITE A MISSION STATEMENT.

People deal with stress better when they have a strong moral compass. This means knowing what you value in life and using that as a guidepost for all decisions. By creating a mission statement people can begin to identify the underlying causes of behaviors, as well as what truly motivates them to change. "A mission statement becomes the North Star for people," says Dr. Groppel. "It becomes how you make decisions, how you lead and how you create boundaries."

Now think about your mind as an emotional muscle. Unrelenting stress without a break will not make it stronger. Your emotions, your brain and your body need moments of recovery to get stronger from stress.

"It's about stress and recovery. Just like you build a physical muscle, just like you build biceps, you have to take the same approach to life stressors,"

stress, our friends and family members are most likely to give us the support we need to get through it.

One of my favorite friendship studies involved a steep hill, a heavy backpack and 34 university students. Students were fitted with a backpack full of free weights equivalent to 20 percent of their body weight. They stood at the base of a hill on the University of Virginia campus with a 26-degree

> **Social support is a defining element in our happiness, quality of life, and ability to cope with stress.**

says Jack Groppel, co-founder of the Johnson & Johnson Human Performance Institute, which offers a course called The Power of Positive Stress.

Think of meditation like high-intensity interval training (HIIT) for the brain. During HIIT, you go as hard as you can, then you give yourself a few minutes of recovery before returning to the exercise. This cycle is repeated multiple times and has been shown to be more effective for building strength than long, slow bouts of exercise.

## SUPPORT AND RELATIONSHIPS
Your friends and family can be both a cause of stress and a cure for it.

### Lean on Loved Ones
The pressure of family responsibilities is one of the most common forms of stress. But during times of

incline. Wearing the heavy backpack, they had to imagine climbing that hill and guess the incline. When a student stood alone, he or she tended to guess that the hill was very steep. But when the student stood next to a friend, the hill didn't look as daunting. Overall, students in pairs consistently gave lower estimates of the hill's incline compared with students who were alone. And the longer the friends had known each other, the less steep the hill appeared.

The lesson: The world does not look as challenging with a friend by your side.

For people who study stress, the role of friendship, family and support networks can't be overstated. Time and again research shows that social support is a defining element in our happiness, quality of life and ability to cope with stress.

## Map Your Social Network

During times of high stress we have a tendency to retreat. We cancel social plans and focus on the work, money crisis or trauma that is our source of stress. But friends and social support are among the best forms of therapy to help you escape stress for brief periods of time. Friends can also make you feel better about yourself, and that mountain of stress in your life won't look so steep.

When Dr. Steven Southwick co-wrote his book on resilience, he interviewed a number of people who had shown resilience against all odds, including former prisoners of war and people who had

to map it out on paper. "Who is in your life? Who can you count on?" asks Dr. Southwick. Make your own list of your social network and keep it handy when you need to call on someone for support.

## Reach Out and Touch Someone

The simple act of touching another person—or being touched—can ease your stress. James A. Coan, an assistant professor of psychology and a neuroscientist at the University of Virginia, recruited 16 women who felt they had strong support in their relationships. To simulate stress, he subjected each woman to a mild electric shock under three conditions, all

> **" Friends and social support are among the best forms of therapy to help you escape stress for brief periods of time.**

survived trauma. One thing they had in common was social support.

"The resilient people we interviewed actively reached out for support," said Dr. Southwick. "They don't sit around and wait."

Even POWs held in isolation devised a tapping method of communication with their fellow prisoners. "Most, if not all, said it was life-saving to know they weren't alone and they were cared for," said Dr. Southwick.

When Dr. Southwick, a psychiatrist, meets with a new patient, one of the first things he does is construct a diagram of the patient's social network. Sometimes they just talk about it; some patients want

while monitoring her brain. The shocks were administered in no particular order while the woman was 1) alone, 2) holding a stranger's hand, and 3) holding her husband's hand.

Notably, both instances of hand-holding reduced the neural activity in areas of the woman's brain associated with stress. But when the woman was holding her husband's hand, the effect was even greater, and it was particularly pronounced in women who had the highest marital-happiness scores. Holding a husband's hand during the electric shock resulted in a calming of the brain regions associated with pain similar to the effect brought about by use of a pain-relieving drug.

## Animals Can Help

Spending time with your pet can offer a temporary reprieve from stress. Spending time with your dog and taking it for a walk is a two-fer—you get the stress reduction of a pet plus the stress-busting benefits of a walk outdoors.

The evidence that pets are a source of comfort and stress relief is compelling. At Veterans Affairs hospitals, therapy animals, including dogs and parrots, have helped patients undergoing treatment for post-traumatic stress to reduce their anxiety.

Studies have shown that after just 20 minutes with a therapy dog, patients' levels of stress hormones drop and levels of pain-reducing endorphins rise.

In a controlled study of therapy dog visits among patients with heart disease, researchers at the University of California, Los Angeles, found a significant reduction in anxiety levels and blood pressure in the heart and lungs in those who spent 12 minutes with a visiting animal, but no such effect occurred among comparable patients not visited by a dog.

## GIVE SUPPORT

If you lead a highly stressful life, the solution may be to add one more task to your daily to-do list: Give back.

Research consistently shows that helping other people and giving social support is a powerful way to manage the stress in your life and boost your resilience. Volunteer work, mentoring, mowing your elderly neighbor's lawn, listening to a friend who is struggling— all these can enhance your own ability to manage stress and thrive.

Coan says the study simulates how a supportive marriage and partnership gives the brain the opportunity to outsource some of its most difficult neural work. "When someone holds your hand in a study or just shows that they are there for you by giving you a back rub, when you're in their presence, that becomes a cue that you don't have to regulate your negative emotion," he told me. "The other person is essentially regulating your negative emotion but without your prefrontal cortex. It's much less wear and tear on us if we have someone there to help regulate us."

# Four Easy(ish) Steps Toward Happiness You Can Take Today

BY TIM HERRERA

## ARE YOU HAPPY?

It's a question we might ask ourselves here and there when something great (or awful) happens to us. But think about it in a general sense: When was the last time you evaluated your overall happiness and satisfaction with life?

There are so many factors to consider when answering that question that it can feel overwhelming or, even worse, become yet another stressor weighing on your happiness. Today we're going to focus on the four things you can do right now(ish) to improve your happiness. Because you deserve it, friends.

## CONQUER YOUR NEGATIVE THINKING

Humans have evolved to focus on the negative. If we overlearn a bad situation, we're more inclined to avoid those situations in the future or react more quickly. But, as we all know, that isn't always helpful in a modern world. When something bad happens, we tend to overanalyze and have trouble getting our mind off it.

The trick to avoiding those spirals and rabbit holes of misery is to acknowledge and challenge our negative thoughts. Rather than try to bury them, we should own those thoughts and ask ourselves a few questions, like "What is the evidence for this thought?" or "Am I basing this on facts or on feelings?" A little self-investigation can help us get over the thoughts that just won't leave our heads otherwise.

## FORGIVE YOURSELF

This one is really simple: Go easy on yourself. If you're compassionate and supportive of other people, why shouldn't you give yourself the same luxury?

This can be a difficult concept for those of us who tend to beat ourselves up over perceived failures, so our guide has an exercise you can use to practice. Write yourself a letter of compassion just as you would to a neighbor or friend who had experienced a hard-ship. The concept is the same, only the recipient is you.

## MONEY HELPS, BUT ONLY TO A POINT

An often-cited study from a few years ago boldly named the amount of money at which happiness peaks: $75,000 per year. Another recent (but less rigorous) examination put that number at $100 million. Still another study said lottery winners are no happier than the rest of us.

Mmm...what?

The truth is, we're plagued by the constant craving for the next thing. Tara Parker-Pope calls this the "hedonic treadmill" in the happiness guide and, essentially, we're stuck on it.

A more helpful way to look at this idea is to find purpose and meaning at work. Rather than focusing on work as a means to earn money, try to find genuine satisfaction and purpose in the work you do. Studies have shown this is possible in every type of job.

## BUY MORE TIME

If given the choice between buying material things and buying services that save you time, you might want to think about the timesavers.

In two surveys cited in our guide to happiness, researchers found that people who spent money on conveniences like ordering takeout for dinner or getting a cab were happier than those who didn't.

So what does that mean for you? If you can afford it, buy yourself some extra time. (Yes, this is permission to order a pizza for dinner tonight.)

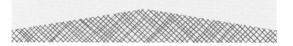

## Thank you...

In reality, this book started long before anyone considered putting these stories in a binding and between its beautifully designed covers. It started with the birth of Smarter Living, and there are many people at *The New York Times* to thank for that.

This whole venture began with Cliff Levy, a supportive, thoughtful editor and mentor whose ingenuity and guidance helped lead the rise of service journalism at the *Times*. To Karron Skog, whose leadership and friendship have allowed us to be inventive and have taught us how to shine as editors. Sarah Graham is an editor anyone would be grateful to have: nimble, sharp, a team player and a solid shoulder to lean on. And, perhaps most of all, we owe our deepest gratitude to the person who connected the dots that created Smarter Living and brought it to life: Justin Bank.

Jas Riyait and Agnes Lee are art directors that editors dream of: creative, innovative and fun. Their vision and creativity elevated Smarter Living in ways we never could have imagined, and without them our stories would not stand apart in the way they do.

Additionally, we need to thank Ben French, Rosy Catanach, Michael Renehan, Sara Bremen-Rabstenek, Joel Stillman, Sooyeon Kim, Alessandra Villaamil, Hilla Katki, August Navarro, Katherine McMahan, Bill French and Matthias Gattermeier of the old "Beta" team who helped to envision our "how-to" guides, make them look beautiful and,

more important, allow them to truly help our readers. Likewise, Smarter Living would not be what it is without the sharp, insightful guidance of Michael Gold, Michelle L. Dozois, Anna Dubenko, Lindsey Underwood, Dagny Salas, Erin Seims, Claudio Cabrera, Eric Bishop, Carla Correa, Talya Minsberg, Ron Lieber, Ashwin Seshagiri, Michael Zhao, Mat Yurow, Korrena Bailie and Taylor Tepper, as well as our colleagues Roberta Zeff, Toby Bilanow, Alan Henry, Kenneth R. Rosen and James Williamson. And thanks to Jody Mak, Johna Paolino, Douglas Back, Andy Creighton, Natalya Shelburne and Yuraima Estevez, of the current Reader Guidance team, who keep pushing the bounds of Smarter Living and how we can make our stories as helpful and useful as possible.

Alex Ward, thank you for your wisdom and patience in shepherding us through the process of creating this book. And to everyone at Black Dog and Leventhal, particularly Lisa Tenaglia, whose vision for this book made it come to life in a way we could have never imagined. Katie Benezra and Joanna Price, you made our copy sing with your amazing eye.

On a personal note, a special "Thank You" to Leron Thumim, a true partner who supports the hard work and time that goes into the job of editing and who makes every aspect of life smarter.

And to Mary Jane Weedman, Streets and Strudel, whose living truly is...the smartest. (Lol.)

# INDEX

## ABOUT THE AUTHORS

**Karen Barrow** is an editor for the Smarter Living team of *The New York Times*. She guides the creation of content that helps people do things a little bit better—from laundry to saving for retirement. Previously, she was one of the founding editors for Well, *The New York Times*'s personal health section, a medical reporter and children's science writer.

**Tim Herrera** is the founding editor of Smarter Living, where he edits and reports stories about living a better, more fulfilling life. Before coming to the *Times,* he was a reporter and digital strategist at the *Washington Post,* and previously he was a metro reporter for *amNewYork* and *Newsday*. He graduated from New York University with degrees in Anthropology and Journalism, and he lives in New York with his platonic life partner, M.J., and their two cats, Strudel and Streets.

**Karron Skog** is an associate managing editor at *The New York Times*. She previously served as the editorial director of Smarter Living, driving journalism that helps readers live better, more enriching lives, and as an editor on several news and features desks.